A JOURNAL OF
CONSCIOUSNESS AND TRANSFORMATION

ReVision

CONTENTS

I0116429

Cover image: Stonehenge, Photo by Astrid Berg

Winter 2010 • Volume 31 • Number 1

What is ReVision?

For almost thirty years ReVision has explored the transformative and consciousness-changing dimensions of leading-edge thinking. Since its inception ReVision has been a vital forum, especially in the North American context, for the articulation of contemporary spirituality, transpersonal studies, and related new models in such fields as education, medicine, organization, social transformation, work, psychology, ecology, and gender. With a commitment to the future of humanity and the Earth, ReVision emphasizes the transformative dimensions of current and traditional thought and practice. ReVision advances inquiry and reflection especially focused on the fields presently identified as philosophy, religion, psychology, social theory, science, anthropology, education, frontier science, organizational tran formation, and the arts. We seek to explore ar cient ways of knowing as well as new models transdisciplinary, interdisciplinary, multicultura dialogical, and socially engaged inquiry. It is o intention to bring such work to bear on what a pear to be the fundamental issues of our time through a variety of written and artistic moda ties. In the interests of renewal and fresh visio we strive to engage in conversation a diversi of perspectives and discourses which have ofte been kept separate, including those identifie with terms such as Western and Eastern; indig nous and nonindigenous; Northern and Souther feminine and masculine; intellectual; practica and spiritual; local and global; young and o

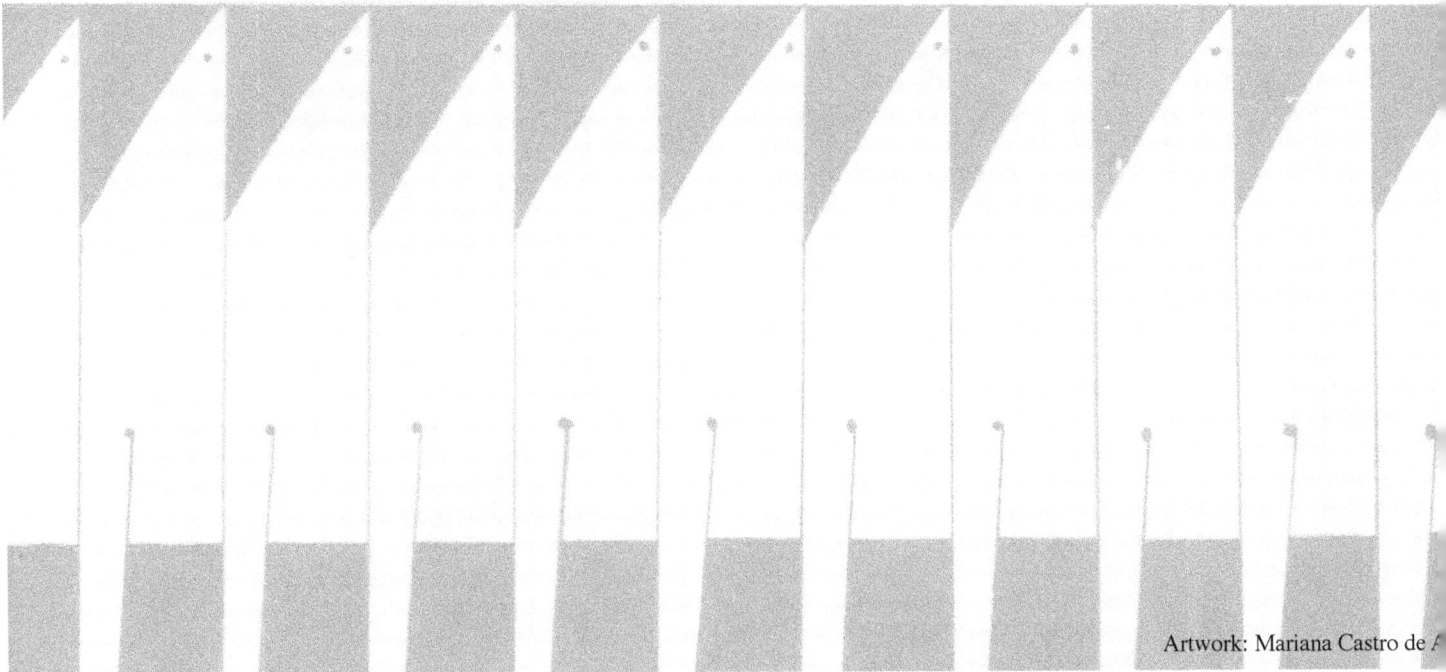

Artwork: Mariana Castro de /

Volume 31, No. 1 (ISBN 978-0-9819706-1-5)

ReVision (ISSN 0275-6935) is published as part of the *Society for the Study of Shamanism, Healing, and Transformation*.

Manuscript Submissions

We welcome manuscript submissions. Manuscript guidelines can be found on our webpage http://revisionpublishing.org.

POSTMASTER: Send address changes to ReVision Publishing, P.O. Box 1855, Sebastopol, CA 95473.

Subscriptions

For subscriptions mail a check to above address or go to www.revisionpublishing.org.

Individual Subscriptions

Subscription for one year: $36 online only, $36 print only (international $72), $48 print and on-line (international $84).

Subscription for two years: $60 online only, $60 print only (international $96), $79 print and online (international $115).

Subscription for three years: $72 online only, $72 print only (international $108), $96 print and online (international $132).

Institutional Subscriptions

$98 online only (international $134), $134 print and online (international $191).

Please allow six weeks for delivery of first issue.

ReVision Abstracts

Vol. 31 No. 1   *Winter 2010*

Berg, A. (2010). Review of Robert Bosnak's *Embodiment: Creative Imagination in Medicine, Art and Travel. ReVision*, *31*(1), 53-55. doi:10.4298/REVN.31.1.53-55

Boznak's book defines a type of dream work in which one works with the dreamer in dual consciousness - the hypnagogic and the waking state. Dream image affects are re-experienced and anchored in the body to be experienced simultaneously.

Coehlo, A. (2010). The erotics of accountability: A psychological approach. *ReVision*, *31*(1), 36-43. doi:10.4298/REVN.31.1.36-43

Accountability is a process that is essential to re-building, healing, and maintaining relationships. Based upon her graduate research, she explores accountability models and insights about psychological barriers to accountability. Considered first is a case that was brought before the South African Truth and Reconciliation Commission, then cultural and religious sources related to accountability. Discussion of various states of victimization provides understanding about difficulties of entering into accountability processes and the necessity for compassionate objectivity in order to work psychologically with states of victimization. Engaging with states of victimization ignites the transformative potentials of accountability practices for those who have caused harm as well as those who have been harmed and the community within which they make their lives.

Herman, L. (2010). Engaging images of evil: An imaginal approach to historical trauma. *ReVision*, *31*(1), 44-52. doi:10.4298/REVN.31.1.44-52

We are vulnerable to the traumatizing possibilities of engaging with the images of historical events of evil whether we receive them through the tales of our forebears or through broadcast to us in their immediacy on the television or Internet. Trauma studies explore our tendencies to destructively repeat undigested personal psychic material and history shows us how collectively we have passionately followed paths no longer relevant to the present. This article explores the author's experience of engaging with the images of Auschwitz. She offers a theory developed from her own and others' experience researching the iconic death camp as to how we might creatively contain horror. Applying an emergent systems approach to the memory of historical trauma, she describes an iterative process for the non-participant to artfully engage the images of evil events.

Jaenke, K. (2010). Soul and soullessness. *ReVision*, *31*(1), 3-18. doi:10.4298/REVN.31.1.3-18

Imaginal Psychology is a newly coalescing orientation within the field of psychology with the soul as its primary concern. While the soul introduces into psychology the presence of mystery, the soul's landscape can be entered through practices that attend to imagination, experience, and affective life. The soul has a passionate nature—the ability to be affected. When the soul loses this ability, there is soul loss and psychic numbing—soullessness. The structure of soullessness is depicted through a six-fold model of concentric layers built around a numb core. The numb core, arising from intolerable experiences of trauma and failure, can become covered by the layers of: shame, defense against shame, shamelessness, evil acts and deception. Restoration of the soul's passionate nature requires travelling back through all the subjective states that constellated around the original numbness. The encounter with soullessness can become an initiatory threshold, in which the soul reclaims soulfulne in response to soullessness.

Loeb, B. (2010). Therapy dreams. *ReVision*, *31*(1), 32-35. doi:10.4298/REVN.31.1.32-35

This piece includes four "Therapy Dreams," stories that are written spontaneously, in a waking state, through a process of active imagination. They show the unfolding psychological development of a client's transference and projections onto a therapist. "Therapy Dream reveals child-like emotional dependency and profound longing for connection with an important, larger-than life being, who is also symbolic of the adult's longing for connection with the true self.

Policar, H. J. (2010). The shadow of the American dream: The clash of class ascension and shame. *ReVision*, *31*(1), 19-31. doi:10.4298/REVN.31.1.19-31

This article explores the hidden shadow of the American dream and its often unexamined underlying tenets of upward mobility, achievement, and materialism that are linked to class identity and shame. The nuances of class identity shame create internal conflict that can only be resolved through acknowledging and experientially turning toward this affect. Turning towards shame requires the safety of a contained space in which the vulnerabilities associated with shame may be touched and transmuted. Thus, those who work most closely with subjective states associated with class identity, including psychologists and educators, must be aware of the cultural taboos against discussing it, and equipped to provide emotionally safe containers that facilitate breaking through the defensive posturing that often covers class shame.

Sabini, M. (2010). The mystery of death: Noble and knowab *ReVision*, *31*(1), 56-62. doi:10.4298/REVN.31.1.56-62

This article explores death as a field phenomenon with accompany reverberations that impact the kinship group of the dying person pr to death in myriad ways: as seemingly irrational concerns and fear unplanned visits to the person, inexplicable utterances, and prescie dreams and visions. The author presents eight cases—sudden and accidental deaths, suicide, murder, near-death, and natural death in old age—and discusses the accompanying reverberations. When the archetypal energy of impending death is contained in a consciously accepted dying process, the field effects on others tend to be milde and easier to comprehend. When death occurs suddenly, its effects can be troubling and/or mystifying. Having the kinship group share experiences arising in the imagination helps make sense of them a deepens the mourning process for all.

Imaginal Psychology

Karen Jaenke, Editor

This issue focuses on imaginal psychology, a newly coalescing orientation to psychology with an ancient taproot. Imaginal psychology stands alongside other major orientations to psychology— cognitive behavioral, depth, humanistic and transpersonal. What is distinctive to imaginal psychology is its care of the soul. The soul expresses itself primarily in images, from whence this orientation derives its name. Some theorists associated with the orientation of imaginal psychology include James Hillman, Thomas Moore, Aftab Omer, Jean Houston, Shawn McNiff, Robert Sardello and Mary Watkins.

Articles in this issue showcase the versatility of imaginal psychology to wrestle with difficult social issues that too often fall off the radar of psychology: soullessness and evil, class identity and shame, accountability in broken relationships where harm and injury have been caused; and collective historical trauma. My opening article, "Soul and Soullessness", unpacks "soul" as the primary concern of imaginal psychology. For those not yet familiar with imaginal psychology, basic theory and practices foundational to imaginal psychology are outlined in the first portion of this article. It then turns to unpack the condition of "soullessness," which

in extreme form becomes evil, i.e. the numbness of the soul or the loss of its passionate nature. The article considers what it means subjectively to encounter soullessness in oneself or another.

Joy Policar examines the hidden shadow of the American dream of class ascension, which can involve internal conflict, underlying shame and defensive posturing. The shame that can accompany class ascension can only be resolved when a safe container is provided to turn toward, acknowledge and transform the vulnerabilities associated with shame. Anne Coelho considers the practice of accountability by looking at the subjective states of victimization that must be addressed in order for a person to accept responsibility for harm caused and harm received. Lisa Herman considers how images associated with collective historical trauma, such as the holocaust, can be engaged through various modalities of imagination by those removed from the historical event but still affected by the event and the images it evokes.

Three additional articles show the close affinity, and sometimes indistinguishable relationship, between imaginal and depth psychology, which share in common a respect for images as carriers of the deep process of the psyche. Barbara Loeb's "Therapy Dreams" showcases the role of waking imag-

ery and the use of active imagination. In series of vignettes, which carry the imaginative flavor of childhood stories, she allows spontaneously unfolding imagery to depict phases in her process of transference onto a therapist to whom she is deeply attached. Meredith Sabini's article "The Mystery of Death: Noble and Knowable" recounts six instances of sudden or accidental death, plus one of natural death in old age, in order to show that what we call "an accident" may be so only from the perspective of the visible, explicate world. Astrid Berg reviews Robert Boznak's book *Embodiment: Creative Imagination in Medicine, Art and Travel* (2007), providing a synopsis of his embodied approach to dream work, which involves anchoring the major images of the dream in the body. Some of the visual images in the issue, including the cover image, are also her photographs. Imagery of portals abound in these pages, suggesting to the eye that images are portals to the soul.

Photo: Astrid Berg, www.astridberg.com

Soul and Soullessness

Karen Jaenke

Imaginal psychology is a newly coalescing orientation within the field of psychology with an ancient taproot. The orientation of imaginal psychology may be situated alongside the four other orientations to psychology: cognitive behavioral, depth, humanistic, and transpersonal. Aftab Omer, a primary voice within imaginal psychology and an important influence of mine, distinguishes these five orientations according to the primary concern of each one (2003).[1]

For cognitive behavioral the original primary concern 80 years ago was behavior, to which mind was added approximately 40 years ago. Within this orientation, the Greek word psyche is often translated as "mind" and psychology as "the study of the mind". Cognitive behavioral psychology, the predominant mainstream orientation, reflects

Karen Jaenke, M.Div., Ph.D., has taught graduate students of psychology and dream studies at Meridian University, formerly known as the Institute of Imaginal Studies and JFK University during the last eight years. A graduate of Princeton Seminary and the California Institute of Integral Studies, her dissertation "Personal Dreamscape as Ancestral Landscape" explored the power of dreams to recover deep memory and indigenous roots. Her approach to human development, soul potential, and the collective dilemmas of our times focuses on the ancient yet neglected resources found in dreams, deep memory, imagination, and the body. She has a coaching, hypnotherapy, and consulting practice in Pt. Reyes, CA.

the biases of the modern cultural context from which it emerged, with its emphasis on cognition and behavior. The other four alternative orientations continue to address certain limitations found within cognitive behavioral psychology, such as its reliance on the hard sciences as the model and standard for the study of the human psyche and its ahistorical nature (Omer, 2003). In becoming established as a modern academic discipline, psychology lost connection to its ancient roots (Omer, 2003).

The primary concern for depth psychology centers on the relationship between the conscious and the unconscious. Within humanistic psychology, the primary concern is personhood, and more specifically, self-actualization and the potential of the person. The primary concern within transpersonal psychology is consciousness, with a focus on altered states of consciousness.

> Depth, humanistic and transpersonal psychology are sister orientations to imaginal psychology; all in their own way, are coming to terms with modernity and recognizing cognitive behavioral psychology as a modern event. Yet depth, humanistic and transpersonal psychology are still constrained by the European conversation.... The relative neglect of indigenous knowledge about soul and soul loss, of myth, ritual and story, is part of the gap [that remains to be bridged]....

Imaginal psychology reclaims soul as psychology's primary concern. The soul expresses itself in images. Care of the soul asks that we play close attention to the images we inhabit. Imaginal psychology has its roots in the transformative practices that are at the core of many spiritual traditions and the creative arts. In the last one hundred years, modern depth psychology has rediscovered these sacred potentials. Imaginal psychology traces this vein of gold through its ancient and modern manifestations in ways relevant to our contemporary lives, enabling a distinctly postmodern psychology to emerge. (Omer & Kremer, 2003, p. 39).

In order to extend its knowledge of the soul, imaginal psychology draws upon a number of knowledge domains, including: spiritual traditions, creative arts, mythology, somatic practices, literary and poetic imagination, mystical philosophy, indigenous wisdom, deep ecology and social critique (Omer, 2003). By drawing upon these knowledge domains, imaginal psychology taps into sources of wisdom and transformative practices that predate the modern period and transcend mainstream psychology's Euro-centric discourse (Omer, 2003). These knowledge domains reflect the reclaiming of the ancient roots of psychology in the modern period and "contribute to the emergence of a postmodern-indigenous orientation to psychology" (Omer & Kremer, 2003, p. 39). Knowledge of the care of the soul can be traced to the shamanic practices of our distant ancestors. "The roots of imaginal psychology are in shamanism, and shamans are its ritual specialists" (Omer & Kremer, 2003, p.40).

As the knowledge domains imply by the inclusion of communal, cultural, societal and ecological perspectives,

versatility of this orientation to address social and cultural issues psychologically is one of its compelling strengths. Other orientations to psychology have too often suffered from entrenchment within Euro-centric and middle or upper-middle class biases. The versatility of this orientation is illustrated in the range of social and cultural issues

accessed and mediated. What occurs when there is a loss of soul, resulting in soullessness, and the requirements for healing it, will be explored after further considering the nature of soul itself.

Soul

Thomas Moore differentiates psychology, "a secular science", from "care of the soul [which] is a sacred art" (1994, xv). With its emphasis on soul, imaginal psychology introduces into psychology something religious.[2] For soul connotes the presence of mystery.

So what is meant by soul? Since soul is a mystery, and hence is neither easily nor precisely defined, it is beneficial to gather several perspectives on the nature of soul.

Imaginal psychology is a newly coalescing orientation within the field of psychology with an ancient taproot.

soul does not belong exclusively to the human individual or human world, but is a more encompassing fabric in which the sacred web of life is held. All forms of life participate in soul. The orientation of imaginal psychology moves towards the recognition that that the entire world is ensouled, hence deserving our respect and the working out of right relationship.

The reclamation of the vision of an ensouled universe also points to "the necessity for the work of the re-animation or reenchantment of human culture" (Omer and Kremer, 2003). Since the modern project has been directed towards demystifying the universe, the post-modern task is of reanimating the universe is a considerable one. The 20th century culminates an era of disenchantment that demonstrates the dire collective consequences—for community, society and the planetary web of life—when the informing presence of soul becomes obscured from shared awareness and action.

While soul is a religious word being reclaimed by imaginal psychology, the

to which it can lend depth of understanding. Examples of its facility in illuminating areas of social concern include the topics of: accountability and reconciliation in relationships where harm has been caused; class identity and shame; historical trauma; and soullessness and evil (all addressed within this issue of ReVision.)

The ability to recognize the presence of soul in both human and non-human realms seems to require awakeness to

Within imaginal psychology, the Greek word psyche is translated not as mind but with its older meaning, as soul. According to James Hillman, "Psyche in the Greek language, besides being soul, denoted a night-moth or butterfly and a particularly beautiful girl in the legend of Eros and Psyche.... Images of the soul show...feminine connotations." (1994, p. 68). Hillman further amplifies the ways of soul, describing soul as a way of knowing that is receptive to the world and as the realm of "imagination, passion fantasy, reflection, that is neither physical and material...nor spiritual and abstract... yet bound to then both. We catch our soul's most essential nature in death experiences, in dreams of the night, and in the images of 'lunacy'" (1992, p. 68). Soul dwells in the realm of experience and "moves

Painting: Karen Jaenke

the presence of soul within oneself. It is through our connection with the informing presence of soul that respect for other forms of ensouled existence is

indirectly in circular reasonings, where retreats are as important as advances" This implies that regressions are as important to the soul's life as progress

sions and hints at a tension between the ways of soul and our culture of progress. Furthermore, "soul is vulnerable and suffers, it is passive and remembers. It is water to the spirit's fire... Soul is imagination, a cavernous treasury" (p. 69). Perhaps most importantly, "The cooking vessel of the soul takes in everything, everything can become soul; and by taking into its imagination any and all events, psychic space grows" (p. 69.) This statement implies that soul carries an inherent largesse, a capacity for ingesting and metabolizing the full range of life's experiences, even difficult and horrific ones, and for creating something of beauty even from the messiness, disappointments, and tragedies of life. As we shall see, it implies that soullessness can be reclaimed, and turned back into soulfulness.

In Care of the Soul, Moore indicates, "Soul is not a thing, but a quality or a dimension of experiencing life. Soul is related to depth, value, relatedness, heart and personal substance" (1994, p. 5). Furthermore, "soul is revealed in attachment, love, and community, as well as in retreat on behalf of inner communing and intimacy" (xi-xii). "Tradition teaches that soul lies midway between understanding and unconsciousness, and that its instrument is neither the mind nor the body but imagination" (xiii). Moore continues,

> Soul is closely connected to fate, and the turns of fate almost always go counter to the expectations and often to the desires of the ego....Soul is the font of who we are, and yet it is far beyond our capacity to devise and control. We can cultivate, tend, enjoy and participate in the things of the soul, but we can't outwit it or manage it or shape it to the designs of a willful ego.... The act of entering into the mysteries of the soul, without sentimentality or pessimism, encourages life to blossom forth according to its own designs and with its own unpredictable beauty. Care of the soul is not solving the puzzle of life [but] an appreciation of the paradoxical mysteries that blend light and darkness into the grandeur of what human life and culture can be (Moore, 1994, p. xviii-xix).

"We care for the soul solely by honoring its expressions, by giving it time and opportunity to reveal itself, and by living life in a way that fosters the depth, interiority and quality in which it flourishes." (p. 304).

Aftab Omer defines soul as "the mysterious stillness, aliveness and otherness at the center of being" (2008). Since soul is infused with mystery, defying positivistic categories and easy defining, he suggests a more fruitful way to approach soul is to consider the portals into the soul. And the prime portal into the soul is imagination; indeed, the name given to this orientation, "imaginal psychology", reflects that imagination and images form a gateway into soul (2003).

Images are primordial to the psyche. Hence Hillman calls the soul's first freedom "the freedom to imagine" and the autonomy of fantasy "the soul's last refuge of dignity, its guarantor against all oppression" (1992, p. 39). The uncensored products of the psyche are images, which appear bare and unveiled in dreams and psychosis alike. As well, all waking experience is governed by the underground flow of imagery. To access this "river of imagination" is to be in touch with the stirrings of soul.[3] Given that "our everyday experiences are infused with the invisible," images offer "the promise of opening us to the invisible part of the Mystery" (Omer & Kremer, 2003, p. 37).

Image is the irreducible element in experience. Conversely, the essence of experience is condensed and carried within images. According to Omer, images "both mediate and constitute experience" (2008). Images are the glue

Photo: Astrid Berg, www.astridberg.com

that cohere the discreet components of experience—sensation, affect and cognition (Omer, personal communication, December 13, 2004). Hence a natural integrative link exists between sensation and image, between affect and image, and between cognition and image. This link is seen clearly in the recovery of repressed traumatic memory, for if one recovers imagery associated with a trauma, one is on the trail of the traumatic experience. In pointing to the metaphoric base of language, Lakoff and Johnson show that cognition too has its roots in the underground river of images (1980).

In addition to the soul's intrinsic mystery, Omer suggests that "the soul thrives on experience" (personal communication, December 13, 2004). It is through engaging with experience that the soul's life flourishes. Omer identifies four dynamisms of experience, according to which one's capacity for experience may be extended into richer degrees of diversity, depth, intensity, complexity, and sensitivity. These four dynamisms of experience are personalizing, embodying, deepening and diversifying (Omer, personal communication, February 12, 2008). Personalizing (as distinct from personifying) refers to owning one's experience (rather than projecting, disclaiming or being unconscious of it.) Embodying entails connecting with the somatic and affective dimensions of experience. Diversifying refers to engaging with more of the range of one's psychological multiplicity. Deepening refers to contacting the mythic dimension of experience.

Opening to imagination risks opening to intensity of experience. So Omer asks, "If the imagination has these intensities, because it is populated by gods and angels, et cetera, what shall we do with all of that?" (Omer & Kremer, 2003, p. 38) The intensities of imagination carry us beyond the personal, into the transpersonal, archetypal and elemental. One approach has been to forbid the intensities of imagination,

> which doesn't work because that intensity appears in a compensatory way, for example as violence. [When] you take away [the intensities of imagination], as modernity has… the option becomes enacting it in a frenzy of violence or some other extreme. Or to suppress and repress it all and go to the pharmaceuticals for our religion. (Omer & Kremer, 2003, p. 38)

Omer suggests another approach that is more constructive:

> The intensities of imagination require a discipline based in imagination which makes room for the intensities of imaginative life….Without ritual, we drown, because ritual, in the sense of imaginative participation in mystery, creates a context for enacting the intensities of the imagination within a container, within a community, with discipline and accountability. (Omer & Kremer, 2003, p. 38)

The intensities of imagination are related to another defining characteristic of the soul, which is its passionate nature (Omer, personal communication, May 15, 2004). Passionate here means access to the passions, to the emotions, to intense subjective states, indeed suffering. The willingness to consciously suffer one's affective responses (in the sense that they arise and we are not in control of their arousal) and to responsibly engage one's passionate nature suggest a life lived soulfully.

The passionate nature of the soul entails "the ability to be affected" (Omer, personal communication, September 18, 2005). The affects are manifestations of the soul's sensitivities, and need to be honored and expressed in order for the soul's life to flow. Conversely, the damming up of emotional life, the repressing of the soul's passionate nature, creates symptoms for the soul. Hence the practice of attending to soul through attending to images, imagination, experience, and affective life is the heartbeat of imaginal psychology.

and shame-humiliation. "Each [affect] may be regarded as a pattern of expression, a specific package of information triggered in response to a particular type of stimulus" (Nathanson, p. 59).

In order to understand the role of affect and emotion in the programming of human beings, Nathanson uses the analogy of hardware, firmware (the pre-written instructions found on chips), and software (1992). In this analogy, the physical body, with its musculature, skeletal structure, organs, nervous system and biochemistry, forms the hardware. The human genetic code that guides human development and metabolism is the firmware program, written permanently into our biological structure. Environmental influences are the software. The drives and affects are

Soul does not belong exclusively to the human individual or human world, but is a more encompassing fabric in which the sacred web of life is held.

The Soul and Affective Life

Given the soul's passionate nature, imaginal psychology places emphasis on affective life. Imaginal psychology partakes of a natural relationship to affect theory; in turn, affect theory lends a scientific, biological basis to the concerns of imaginal psychology. Donald Nathanson, one affect theorist in a now wide literature on the affects and emotions, writes: "Despite our view of ourselves as thinking beings, cognition is but a frail craft floating on a sea of emotion" (1992, p. 47). This sea of emotion, our affective life, can be differentiated into nine biological affects, which have been observed cross-culturally and documented by Silvan Tompkins as having a physiological, biochemical and neurological basis in the programming of the human species. These nine biological affects may be sub-divided into the positive affects of interest-excitement and enjoyment-joy; the neutral or reset button affect of surprise-startle; and the six negative affects of fear-terror, distress–anguish, anger-rage, dissmell, disgust

part of the firmware system, while "the intricate medley of experiences [form] the software of human life" (p. 28-29).

The terms affect and emotion are used with distinct meaning among affect theorists. While the affects are about unvarying physiological mechanisms, emotion relates to a situation, scene, script or story in which a biological affect is triggered. Affect refers to the physiological portion of emotion; emotion refers to the layering of affect with biographical scripts. In the simplest shorthand, affect is associated with biology while emotion is associated with biography. Affects become emotion as they are loaded up with the script formed through actual life experiences. Thus, while our emotional responses derive from the programming of the innate biological affects, they develop their unique nuance and personal character based on scripts developed in early life and elaborated through the layering of experiences across the course of a lifetime. Affects are modified by personal history and socialization, by nurturance and trauma. Affect is the physiological arousal that then is interpreted in different ways by different cultures.

The affects and affect theory carry a foundational role in Omer's articulation of imaginal psychology, Imaginal Transformation Praxis.[4] In theory and practice, Omer emphasizes the necessity for the expression of affects. Since the affects constellate and carry psychic energy, this psychic energy must go somewhere. And there are three basic options for where this psychic energy can go. Affects can be enacted, somaticized or expressed (Omer, personal communication, March 3, 2005). For the first option, Omer uses the term 'reactive enactment' which means to enact the affect outwardly, often referred to as 'acting out'. To somaticize the affects is to enact them inwardly. The third option, expression, refers to 'expression with awareness'. Among these basic options, the optimal response is expression with awareness, for expression with awareness is the lynchpin for transmuting the affects and for the soul's development into maturity.

The necessity for the expression of the affects is one of the trickiest places for practice within imaginal psychology. While the affects call for and require expression, the irresponsible or uncontained expression of emotion can easily do damage in our relationships. The old cultures recognized that situations that stirred intense emotional responses, such as significant loss, conflict, and major life transitions (puberty, marriage, entrance into a profession, death) require a ritualized structure in order to be negotiated psychologically. Imaginal psychology recognizes the necessity of ritualizing, drawing in significant ways upon an ancient intuitive knowing about the human need for ritual. Ancient ritual practices inform postmodern ritualizing, as living ritual must serve the needs of the present (Anne Coelho, personal communication, February 28, 2009).

However, though necessary to the soul's wellbeing, it is not sufficient for the soul's development simply to find safe havens and ritual containers for the expression of the affects. The affects carry libido, or psychic energy, that can be developed and channeled in creative ways. It is through this funneling of affective arousal into creative forms that the soul individuates and reaches maturity.

One of the cornerstones of Omer's

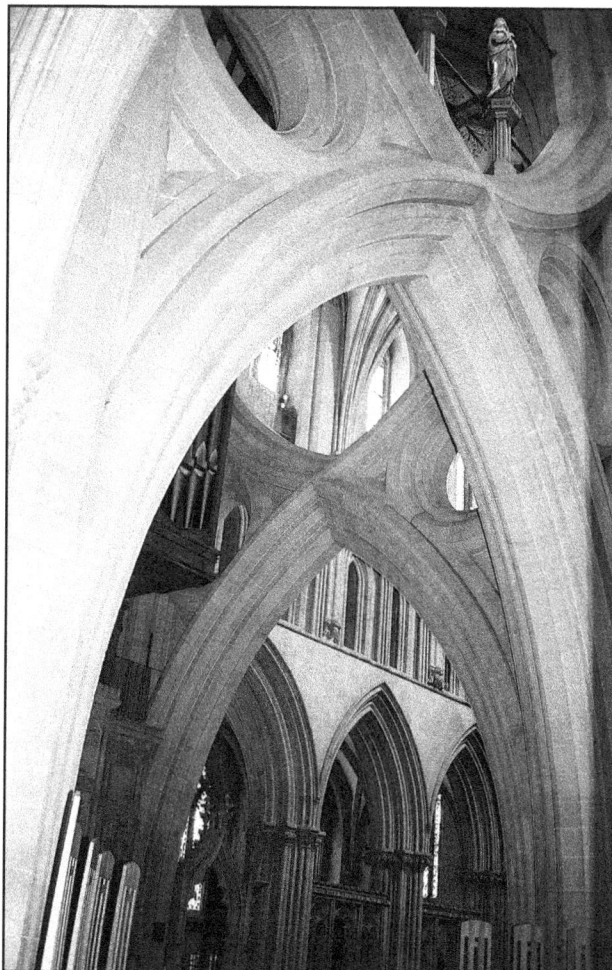

Photo: Astrid Berg, www.astridberg.com

theory and practice concerns the transmutation of the affects into human capacities. For Omer, the four primary negative affects transmute into key human capacities. Grief transmutes into compassion, fear into courage, anger into fierceness (or the right use of force), and shame into humility, dignity, integrity, autonomy, and/or conscience (Omer, personal communication, March 13, 2002). In addition, it seems that disgust transmutes into discernment. "A capacity is a distinct dimension of human development and human evolu-

tion that delineates a specific potential for responding to a domain of life experience (e.g., Compassion responds to Suffering; Courage responds to Danger; Destinicity responds to the Future; Dignity responds to Failure; Fierceness responds to Injustice; Faith responds to Uncertainty; Reflexivity responds to Personal Identity, and so on.)" (Omer, 2008). Another older term for the capacities is human virtues.

To transmute means to take the psychic energy provided by the affect and imaginatively channel it into creative expression in a way that meets the requirements of the present moment. Omer calls this reflexive participation, which he defines as "the practice of surrendering through creative action to the necessities, meanings and possibilities inherent in the present moment" (2008). Reflexivity, or self-awareness, is central to the transmuting of affects, the cultivation of capacities and the process of individuation. Omer defines reflexivity as "the capacity to engage and be aware of the psychological structures that shape and constitute our experience", and he calls reflexivity "the transmuting agent" (2008).

In what arenas are the affects transmuted and the capacities cultivated? Communal contexts that engage and cultivate transformative practices become sites for the development of human capacities. Contexts that both evoke strong affective experience and provide practices for working with intense subjective states especially support capacity building. Rituals have historically provided a container for the expression and transmutation of affects. For example, rituals of mourning assist with the expression and transmutation of grief; rituals of intimacy assist with the expression and transmutation of fear; rituals of conflict assist with the expression and transmutation of anger; and rituals of accountability assist with the expression and transmutation of shame. Transformative practices such as role-playing and imaginal dialogue offer a means for working on identity and developing reflexivity.

For Omer, it is "the emergence of [these] human capacities in a unique and connected way" which defines individuation (2008). The capacities are cultivated through transformative practices, and tend to emerge concurrently; one who develops an abundance of these capacities becomes an empowered person. For Omer, "authentic power (or Soul Power or the Power of Being) refers to the spectrum of human capacities and qualities that are responsive to various domains of life experience in ways that engender truth, beauty, and justice. Authentic Power emerges through enduring and transmuting the vulnerabilities we experience when we turn towards the sensitivities that embody the soul's passionate nature" (2008). One who develops an accumulation of capacities, based on the transmutation of the negative affects, becomes capable of bringing cultural leadership. We most clearly recognize the development of these human capacities in outstanding leaders throughout history, including those of the last century, such as Gandhi, Martin Luther King, Mother Teresa, Nelson Mandela, Harvey Milk, and more immediately, Barack Obama.

Dreams in the Economy of the Soul

My own approach to imaginal psychology has been informed, both intuitively and experientially, by my dream life. Across two decades, dreams have sought me out like a persistent lover. Dreams bring direct transmission of the soul's life; they are a primary teacher concerning the life and ways of soul. Through the prism of dreams, we glimpse the soul's life exposed and laid bare.

Dreams offer rich condensations of experience; a single image gathers and compresses many facets and layers into its net. The roots of the word symbol,

which derives from Greek *symbolon*, convey this well: *sym*, meaning 'together', and *bolon*, meaning 'that which has been thrown', thus 'that which has been thrown together' (Edinger, 1974). The complexity of experience loaded into even a single dream image can be astounding.

Because a single dream typically compiles a series of images, dreams convey especially intense and dense distillations of experience. Indeed, waking

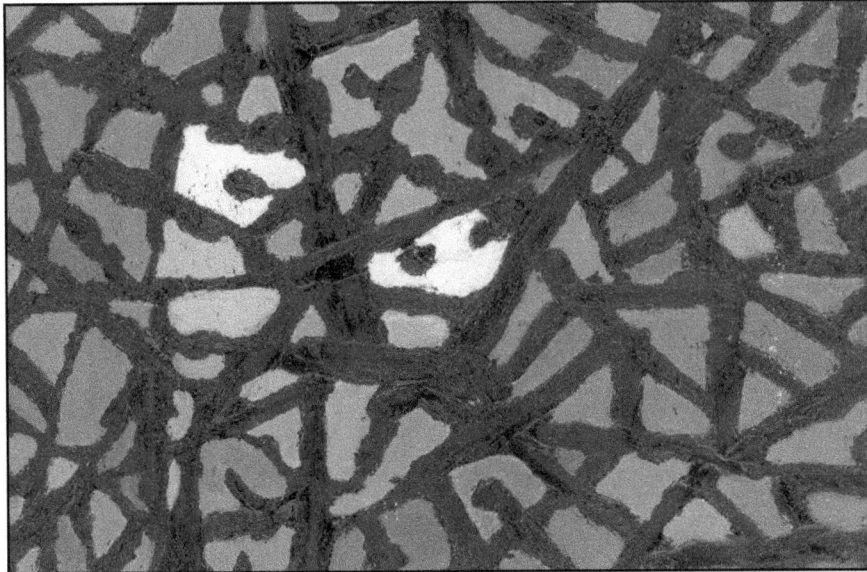

Painting Karen Jaenke

experiences may not match the intensity of experience found with dreams. By actively engaging with the concentrated packets of image and energy compressed within dreams, our capacity for depth, intensity and diversity of experience expands; the soul's life grows. Additionally, dreams provide "maps of the soul's unfolding", serving as daily personal guides sent to further the unfolding of the soul.[5]

Working with dreams as a transformative practice means surrendering to, actively engaging, and metabolizing the affects and deeper soul truths transmitted through dream images. This imagery has its own language, its own grammar, which the would-be seeker must learn—a language based on analogy, associational logic, and affective charge.

We can observe a personifying tendency in the operations of dreams, where all manner of subjective states and psychological dynamics are con-

veyed through the personal dimension, that is, through the persons appearing in our dreams. Hillman refers to the personifying tendency of the soul as "a mode of thought which takes an inside event and puts it outside, at the same time making this content alive, personal and even divine" and as a way of "experiencing the world as a psychological field, where persons are given with events, so that events are experiences that touch us, move us, appeal to us" (1975, p. 12-13).

Even the most apparently inanimate aspect of a dream can be personified through a technique employed in the waking state, that involves giving voice to every aspect of a dream, whether deemed animate or inanimate. Stephen Aizenstat suggests that all images are animate, alive, ensouled (2009). By giving voice and speaking as each aspect of the dream, by personifying, we engage and express the distinct psychic energy carried by each image. In this way, the soul comes to know its inherent multiplicity and vitality through a process of animation and personification.

When undertaken as an ongoing practice, a disciplined commitment to engage dream imagery will necessitate facing the dark and difficult aspects of the soul's life. I recall a dream in which my mother beheaded my father, and arrived on the scene in their bedroom initially wanting to place his head back on his body, before realizing that this was a finished act that could not be reversed. Dreams are infamous for digging up such taboo scenes. They seem to have a special penchant for showing the unacceptable, embarrassing and forbidden sides of life, stripping us of our most cherished self-images while bestowing images of higher potential that exceed grandiose self-imaginings. Dreams act as the soul's system of checks and balances, providing a constant check on our waking self-perceptions, both deflating and expanding our waking self-perceptions. When we wish to see only the positive in a situation, they reveal hidden, more sinister sides lurking at the shadowy edges. When we are fixated on the negatives in a situation, they reveal invisible possibilities.

Perhaps most importantly, dreams, like fate, defy our ability to control. They rise up within us, in their most unpredictable manner, using the tactics of surprise, shock, and intensity of affect to gain our attention. Combining disparate, bizarre and taboo imagery is a favorite tactic of the dream. In all this activity, they break through the narrowing clutches of identity, insisting on surrender to a much greater force— the natural, untamed pure life force. The life force, as channeled through compelling images, heightened affective charge, and the release of psychic energy, is the raw dynamism of the soul unleashed—the most potent force with which we can seek relationship.

Soullessness

The presence of soul within embodied life implies its opposite, namely, the potential for soullessness. To discuss soul without simultaneously keeping an eye out for soullessness, in oneself and others, is to fall into the shadow of soul. Soullessness refers to the possibility of being cut off from soul, of acting against the informing presence of soul. There are a variety of ways to be caught by soullessness. Indifference to the soul's passions in oneself or others, or attending certain passions while neglecting others, are manifestations of soul loss.[6] Soullessness is reflected in the inability to be affected, the inability to access and act upon the soul's sensitivities. A 'hardened heart' and 'heart of stone' are biblical terms for this phenomenon. Similarly, Native peoples recognize the condition of soul loss, and the necessity of soul retrieval. Apathy and ongoing depression reflect an enervation of life's passion. Dissociation, which refers to a splitting in the psyche causing symptoms, is a clinical term that implies being cut off from the

passionate life of the soul.[7] When dissociation becomes culturally pervasive and comes to be taken as normal, there is a collective disconnection from the passionate life of the soul, referred to as normative dissociation.

Lifton's concepts of psychic closing off and psychic numbing are parallel psychological terms for the type of soullessness considered here. Observing the survivors of Hiroshima, he writes: "when human beings are unable to remain open to experience of this intensity [immersion in death] for any length of time, [they...] undergo a process of psychic closing-off; that is, they simply cease to feel. They [have] a clear sense of what [is] happening around them, but their emotional reactions [are] unconsciously turned off" (Lifton, 1969, p. 31-32). While psychic closing-off refers to a transient process, when it extends over days or months into something more lasting, it becomes psychic numbing. The "closing off process [is] a means of creating emotional distance between [oneself] and the intolerable world immediately around" (p. 34). "Conditions like the 'vacuum state' or 'thousand-mile stare' may be thought of as apathy, but are also profound expressions of despair: a severe and prolonged psychic numbing in which the survivor's responses to his environment are reduced to a minimum—often to those necessary to keep him alive—and in which he feels divested of the capacity either to wish or will." (p. 87).

At the far extreme end of the spectrum, soullessness can evolve into evil, which arises when the condition of soul loss is identified with and acted upon in calculated ways. Peck defines evil "as the exercise of political power—that is, the imposition of one's will upon others by overt or covert coercion—in order to avoid extending oneself for the purpose of nurturing spiritual growth" (Peck,

2003. p. 278). "[T]he evil attack others instead of facing their own failures. Spiritual growth requires the acknowledgement of the need to grow. If we cannot make that acknowledgement, we have no option except to attempt to eradicate the evidence of our imperfections" (p. 74). A refusal to respect the autonomous and unfolding nature of the soul, in oneself or the other, marks the

Soullessness can evolve into evil, which arises when the condition of soul loss is identified with and acted upon in calculated ways.

slide into evil.

Evil manifestations of soullessness can appear in the calculated strategizing to control or possess others. Mind control refers to a broad range of psychological tactics that subvert an individual's control of one's own thinking, behavior, emotions, or decisions; mind control theory illuminates this dark phenomenon.[8] Given the soul's expressive nature, the need to control interpretations and expressions of truth are markers of soullessness. Additionally, lies and distortions of the truth, told to protect injured and vulnerable sectors of psyche from exposure and the light of awareness, are manifestations of soullessness.

The Language of Soul

Metaphor-rich language, evocative imagery, mythic motifs, and poetry belong to the language of soul. To adopt the language of soul is a potent thing. This potency is due to the way that the language of soul calls deeply to us. Something within the soul is stirred when soul language is spoken. The language of soul slips past rational constructs and defensive barriers and appeals to something deep and inalienable within. The language of soul reverberates and touches a profound longing within the soul to be addressed in its native tongue.

A particular danger accompanies the use of soul language. The language of soul is potent and seductive, and can be subtly used in ways that mask the true and deeper movements of soul. Those who possess special facility with soul language can be especially vulnerable to abusing it. Those who are facile and clever in their use of soul language, and marry this cleverness to power-seeking agendas stemming from wounded, soul-less places, are especially seductive and dangerous. When the potent language of soul is coupled with the intent to deceive or control others, something evil has begun to assert itself. When

and expressivity can, however, be disrupted by intense and overwhelming experiences which a person is not yet developmentally able to metabolize. A human possibility for numbness exists whenever the soul is insufficiently developed to tolerate the intense affects evoked by life. Experiences of failure that are shamed, of trauma, and of soul-lessness in others tend to trip, or even rip, the young soul. Such experiences can overwhelm the developing soul, short-circuiting its natural propensity

soul. As a symptom, numbness also belongs to the soul's life.

Yet in speaking about soul and soul-lessness, there is also a conceptual danger in generating a dichotomy between soul and soullessness. Paradoxically, soul encompasses soullessness. Indeed, many paradoxical things belong to the soul.

Let us consider two types of experience that often lead to the development of numb places in the soul — trauma and shame. In today's fast-paced,

Despite human claims to mammalian warm-bloodedness, calculating human cold-bloodedness provides a far more terrifying specter than reptilian cold-bloodedness.

the language of soul is married to egoic power drives, the outcomes can be treacherous.

There are both political and spiritual instances of the union of soul language with ego-aggrandizing actions. An extreme example is Hitler, who employed mythic motifs and archetypal imagery to mobilize masses for destructive and genocidal purposes. The younger George Bush offers a recent example of adopting Christian images and themes of good and evil to generate fear-based support for his policies. In addition to political examples, history is replete with spiritual teachers who exploit the language of soul among seekers hungry for spiritual truth.

In contrast, the authentic movements of soul tend to travel in the landscape of vulnerability and transparency. The soul balks at coercion, at distorted or abusive uses of power, and at silencing of its expressive nature. Hence, a culture of secrecy produces a profound burden for the soul. Repressive systems stifle the soul's autonomous and expressive nature.

Experiences Leading to Soullessness

As noted, the human soul develops through expanding its range and capacity for depth and intensity of experience, and by growing its ability to translate its emotional responses into creative action. This natural growth toward increased affective sensitivity

towards growth. When this happens, the soul develops symptoms.

Symptoms are soul's way of expressing. Symptoms express the underlying condition or situation of the soul—generally a condition or situation that has thus far received insufficient attention. Symptoms express something in the soul's life that needs to be attended to; they are also the soul's way of commanding that attention. For the suffering that accompanies symptoms tends to mandate one's attention. Then it becomes necessary to sit with the images and work with the symptoms so that soul's deepest meanings can be uncovered and manifested. To instead literalize an image puts one in danger of enacting the symptom, when what is called for is to receive the messages and meanings carried by the images and symptom. To literalize the images associated with the soul's symptoms is to risk enacting evil (Anne Coelho, personal communication, February 28, 2009).[9]

It is part of soul's passionate nature to have symptoms that are not interesting or passionate, but they're a way of soul trying to find expression under certain restrictive or weird circumstances (Anne Coelho, personal communication, February 28, 2009). Numbness is one such symptom; it is a protective, adaptive response. Numbness is a particular manifestation of a symptomatic

high-stimulus world, many are coping with a steady stream of overwhelming experience. Trauma is another word for overwhelming experience. The psyche's native response to overwhelm is to shut down. Ordinary people who have suffered early, chronic or severe trauma will inevitably have numb sectors within the psyche. In fact, this is a relatively common phenomenon. These are places in the soul where the capacity for feeling, for experiencing the soul's passionate nature, is injured and restricted. Through the prick of trauma, and the defensive-protective system activated in response to trauma, the soul's natural ability to be affected can turn cold, shrivel, and atrophy, leading to a haunting absence of experience. Yet it is out of soul's passionate nature that symptoms arise that are soul's way of seeking healing. Trauma may also create heightened sensitivity to certain experiences.

"When people are overwhelmed and cannot successfully defend themselves, they often feel ashamed" (Levine, 1997, p. 180). In addition, in the course of daily life, we all have experiences of inadequacy and failure which become covered and layered in shame. A supportive environment allows us to integrate experiences of failure in a positive way, to harvest the learnings from our failures. Shame is amplified when experiences of failure in competence and integrity occur outside the context of a supportive environment. A sense of failure can accompany the inability to inhabit one's full affective experience and to translate one's affective responses into empowered, creative action. (Obviously, the young soul is susceptible to many such moments, both because of because it of its nascent state of development and the power differentials it constantly encounters in the world.) It may be useful in this context to distinguish between primary shame (experiences of shame that constitute primary wounding during one's upbringing) and secondary shame (shame that gets triggered as a consequence of the primary shame wound).

As one of the nine biological affects, shame has a physiological basis with a somatic component. Shame is one of the most excruciating experiences to tolerate. If there is not a supportive environment of love, compassion, and care to meet our sense of incompetence and failure, a safe place to acknowledge these vulnerabilities in the presence of an empathic other or empathic community, then the soul develops defensive patterns to cover over these shamed places. Nathanson identifies four defensive responses to shame: attack self, attack other, avoidance and withdrawal (1992). When the attack-other strategy becomes habitual, a false sense of power can be fabricated, as in the chronic use of bullying or intimidation strategies. This false power can feed off of diminishing and dishonoring the free and autonomous other. It contrasts with authentic personal power, rooted in the human capacities of courage, fierceness, compassion, humility and autonomy.

The Symptom of Numbness[10]

While psychic numbing is always a potential within the soul, it is antithetical to the soul's passionate nature. Numbness produces a deadening quality or response to life. Because numbness—a loss of feeling and passion—runs contrary to the soul's deeper nature, places of numbness often become covered in shame. Both numbness and shame involve a turning away from experience. Shame can both precede and follow numbness; numbness can both result from shamed experience and become covered in shame.

Another possibility is that numbness

becomes associated with shamelessness. In this scenario, numbness draws upon the life force from soul to more fully inhabit and protect a numb position. Paradoxically, numbness can enlist the soul's passionate nature to defend or enact its position. (An analogy is cancer in the body, where cancer cells actively reproduce, akin to normal cells, yet these cancer cells feed on, suffocate, and ultimate kill the greater life force of the organism.) Defending or enacting numbness moves one deeper into soullessness. People can enact numbness passionately, fighting tooth and nail to hold onto numbness. When numbness is passionately enacted, there is movement towards evil (Anne Coelho, personal communication, February 28, 2009).

An alternative to enlisting passion in defense of numbness is to bring passionate interest to attend to numbness. When we develop curiosity towards numbness, the coldness of numbness and the heat of passion can interact, and a quickening can occur. When numbness is consciously related to, that is, greeted with awareness, the passion of life is breathed back into soul.

Thus, the vulnerability associated with the soul's passions can either be

opened to or defended against. The soul's passionate nature can be channeled for opposite purposes. When there is inadequate discernment and awareness, the soul's passion will be tapped towards evil. When passion is accompanied with awareness, we move towards goodness, justice, beauty, and truth (Anne Coelho, personal communication, February 28, 2009).

The Structure of Soullessness

In seeking to understand a phenomenon as inchoate as soullessness, it may be helpful to depict it through a model that, like all models, oversimplifies a complex reality in service of greater clarity. This model depicts soullessness as a layering process that builds up

through successive strata that progressively distance an individual from the soul's deeper sensitivities.

The deep structure of soullessness might be pictured as a ball composed of concentric layers that form around a dense core. At the dense core of soullessness is numbness, the absence of feeling. The behaviors and acts that arise from this numbness can be pictured as an outer, visible ring of the ball. Between the numb core and the outer ring of observable behaviors are three additional concentric rings. Immediately surrounding the numb core is the memory of the intolerable experience that evoked the numbing response; typically, these are experiences of overwhelm and trauma, shamed failure and inadequacy. Surrounding and covering these intolerable experiences often is a ring of shame, the affect that arises in response to the failure and the inadequacies of the self. Surrounding the shame layer are the defenses against shame—attack self, attack other, avoidance, and withdrawal. These defenses against shame can manifest in observable behaviors.

Finally, it is possible that a person seeks to cover-up one's shameful,

Soullessness refers to the possibility of being cut off from soul, of acting against the informing presence of soul.

defensive, indifferent actions arising from numbness through secrecy and deception. A layer of deceit can emerge to cover the behavioral acts that emanate from the condition of numbness. Thus, in this model, the concentric layers that form soullessness, arranged from innermost to outermost, are: the numb core; the memory of intolerable experiences such as trauma and failure; shame; defense against shame, indifferent or cruel behavioral and psychological acts; calculated use of deception.

From this six-tier model, we get a sense of the dense layers of experience that collect around soullessness. Normally the layers that make up soullessness (numbness, trauma/inadequacy, shame, defense against shame, acts of indifference, deception) drop below the threshold of consciousness and conscience. Numb sectors in the psyche are heavily barricaded from awareness. In fact, numb places are among the most deeply buried places in the psyche. In addition to being deeply buried, they are usually heavily defended.

minating through imagery the psychological process of engaging with numb sectors. It reveals what is required to metabolize the numb core of soullessness, where the soul's passionate nature has been obscured, deadened. Like the meeting with all numb states, the dream required a disciplined effort to turn

size to non-threatening impotence. Then the body is pieced back together, much smaller, and with its life force to be of manmade proportions.

I am horrified to witness this mechanical operation, which is performed swiftly, as the crocodile can only survive piecemeal for a brief time. The calcula-

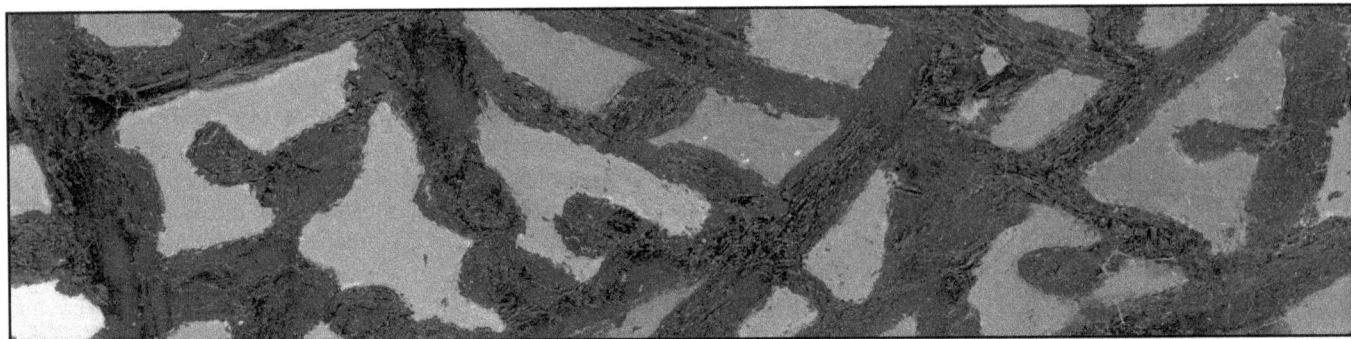

Painting (detail): Karen Jaenke

To restore the soul's deeper passionate nature requires traveling back through all the psychological landscapes that have constellated around the original numbness. Given the successive layering of difficult experiences that surround numbness, we can infer that arduous and complex psychological work is entailed in turning toward soullessness in oneself. It is quite a psychological feat to turn consciously toward one's own soullessness, inclusive of its behavioral manifestations and the defensive, shamed, traumatized, and numb layers from which it emanates. Still, unpeeling each layer in the presence of awareness is necessary for the restoration of experience and re-awakening of the soul's passionate nature.

Soullessness in Oneself

Generally, the encounter with soullessness in oneself is a radically different process than the encounter with soullessness in the other. To consciously engage soullessness in oneself is to peel off each of these layers, by bringing them back into conscious awareness. Among the most elusive of these is the numbness that forms at the core of soullessness.

A dream of mine illustrates the processes of psychic numbing and the conscious turn towards numb places. This dream exposes a place of numbness within the landscape of the soul, illu-

toward, as if the numbness, a complete absence of feeling, was sprayed in a layer of repellent. A natural tendency to turn away from the imagery of numbness in half-conscious disgust first must be overcome. The dream was as follows:

I am living in a room in a spacious old mansion built by a successful industrial baron from the late 19th century. There is a pond and swamp area on the grounds. My car has been driven into the swamp, where it is slowly sinking and submerging.

A crocodile surfaces, crawling out of the swamp. Those of us standing nearby immediately ascend the long stairs leading to the second floor of the mansion, heading towards safety.

I watch from on high at the dining room windows, in shock, as a whole mechanistic system for dealing with the crocodiles swings into operation. Crane-like equipment is used to capture and remove the crocodile from the water, then position and restrain his body on a stone-laid patio below. Chainsaw-like machinery, saws with serrated blades, drop down from above at several angles, then begin cutting and severing the crocodile body into parts. Without any human present, the crocodile body is mechanically cut into sections – tail, torso, snout, legs, hands, feet. Next, segments of flesh are removed from each section, reducing the body

tion and cruelty behind this mechanical approach, executed at a distance from on high—not an outright killing, but shearing his body and rendering the life force of manmade proportions to the point of impotence—is chilling to witness.

Just as the operation is nearly complete, several women swimming in the pond can be seen thrashing in the water. I awake with certainty that the entire operation will be repeated, until any and all threat to humans has been eliminated.

Afterwards I wrote: "Accompanying the image of losing my car in a bog, I sink into layers of numbness, where there is no feeling, especially in my lower body. Contacting the numb places in the body is intensely disturbing, as they seem inhuman, stone-like, the presence of Medusa. In this place, there is no attachment to anyone or anything, just stone coldness. Feeling into my coldness and non-attachment is itself chilling. The burying of the car seems related to letting go of the body I have traveled in during the last 15 years" [the period of owning the car].

In this dream, crocodiles, our reptilian ancestors, represent cold-bloodedness, offering an image of numbness.[11] We tend to contrast reptilian cold-bloodedness with mammalian warm-bloodedness, the latter referring to our capacity for feeling, especially empathic feeling.

for others. Mammalian warm-bloodedness relates to our passionate nature. However, the dream instead fixes on the human capacity for cold-bloodedness.

Human cold-bloodedness manifests through the distinctly human application of technology and through a distancing, mechanical approach to the life of the other. In the dream, human cold-bloodedness, as expressed through the power of the machine, turns against reptilian cold-bloodedness. Machinery, an expression of human ingenuity, is utilized in unfeeling cruel ways. Machines can be operated from a distance, without any witnessing human presence, making it possible to detach and dissociate emotionally from one's cruelty.

Two types of cold-bloodedness are depicted in the dream, the cold-bloodedness of the natural world found in the reptilian body, and the cold-bloodedness of the human, as expressed through the power of the machine. These two types of cold-bloodedness become pitted against one another. In this match, human cold-bloodedness prevails over reptilian cold-bloodedness. Human cold-bloodedness is here revealed as a complex phenomenon that includes the creativity and ingenuity of invention, technology, mechanical application, calculation, detachment, distancing dissociation, and unfeeling cruelty. Despite human claims to mammalian warm-bloodedness, calculating human cold-bloodedness provides a far more terrifying specter than reptilian cold-bloodedness.

The mechanical, calculating, cold-blooded human offers a more sinister human self-image than the ones we normally inhabit. And yet the current state of the planet, and the widespread extinction of species whose blood is on human hands, occurring at a scale and rate difficult to fathom, confirm a lurking human potential for cruelty. The crocodile dream appeared shortly after viewing a disturbing video clip depicting the netting and slaughter of dolphins, their bloody carcasses being chained to the back of trucks and dragged through dusty streets towards processing plants.

Psychologically speaking, the dream depicts a promising process of dismembering the cold-blooded numbness within the self. The crocodile body of cold-bloodedness is dismembered, taken apart, reduced in size and power, then re-membered. This dismemberment/re-memberment process is archetypal in nature, and ultimately hopeful. Dismemberment conveys the most extreme and radical means for addressing a psychological complex—its severing and division into constituent parts, release of its energy and power, followed by re-constitution into a new form. Piercing and dismembering the cold-blooded, unfeeling numb core is necessary to restore the soul's passionate nature.

What is the process by which the numbness at the core of soullessness thaws? To allow this numbness into awareness, to make conscious contact with numbness, requires actually feeling the numbness. Though it may sound like a contradiction, numbness only thaws through awareness and presence.

Initially, to make the bridge of conscious contact between awareness and numbness is to be affected by the chill of what has been held outside awareness, like a person who opens the door to the outdoors on a windy, bitter cold day and is greeted by a brisk breeze. Awareness must first tolerate the chilling and repellent quality of the frozen numbness. However, feeling the numbness, remaining present to numbness, catalyzes a quickening within the soul. Awareness meeting numbness constitutes the beginning of a reversal, where the capacity for feeling and sensitivity begins to pour into a barren or atrophied place within the soul. As the warmth

of feeling penetrates the cold chill of numbness, an alchemical quickening within the soul brings feeling back to life, like a beam of sun shining intently on a patch of frozen ground. One's capacity for feeling is extended; some of the passionate life of the soul is aroused, quickened and restored.

Numbness in the Body

Numb places in the psyche have their counterparts in the body. Numbness is anchored in the body, through frozen, contracted places. Density would be another word for this phenomenon, and in mythology it may be represented by the most dense matter ordinarily encountered, the stones. Medusa is a good mythological exemplar of this frozen energy. In the myth, Medusa transmits her own petrification to others through the cold gaze of her eyes. Perseus, who slays her by beheading her, is not able to meet the direct gaze of eyes. He performs the so-called feat of slaying her using the reflection of his shield in order to see her. Yet to release, rather than attack and kill, the petrifying energy of Medusa requires a different approach that is non-defensive, namely the ability to meet her gaze directly.

The word "petrify", with its double meanings of 'to turn to stone' and 'to be terrified', offers an etymological clue concerning the fear/terror that lives at the core of numbness. The fact that Western culture has not evolved this myth to a different outcome that can preserve Medusa's life and restore her to the human community indicates that the culture has not yet learned to meet the freezing response to terror.

When neither fight nor flight are available as responses to the trauma, freezing becomes the third alternative. In trauma, the tremendous somatic energies mobilized in the fight/flight adrenaline surge response, estimated to be many times that of orgasm, instead become backed up and frozen in the body and nervous system. This is the physiology that underlies the psychology of numbness.

The 20th century culminates an era of disenchantment that demonstrates the dire collective consequences—for community, society and the planetary web of life—when the informing presence of soul becomes obscured from shared awareness and action.

A trauma to a particular part of the body may constellate a numb zone where awareness of sensation no longer flows in free channels of communication. When numbness is constellated in the body, it seems that the neural pathways leading to and from these tissues are disrupted, so that the messages that would normally send and receive are blocked within the numb zone. It is this blocking of awareness of bodily sensation that allows for dissociation from the body to happen. The deepest work in releasing numbness is somatic. In order to garner this release, awareness must stand alongside numbness, as a patient, compassionate witness, until an

rare phenomenon to be allowed direct entrance into the more interior shamed, traumatized, and numb sectors of soullessness within another. As these are among our most protected and guarded places, special trust or extraordinary circumstances seem necessary in order for these inner layers to be exposed to the observing presence of another. Often it is an earned privilege. In the best scenario, where trust runs deep and the container to hold suffering is strong, psychotherapy offers one protected context where shame, trauma and unfeeling can be uncovered, metabolized, and transformed.

But instead of these tender places,

and deceit that collect around the commission of evil acts generates a climate of skewed perception, deception, and subterfuge.

The attempt to cover up past evil can require new acts of evil, accompanied by new levels of demonic deceit. The tendency towards escalation of evil through increasing layers of deception seems to occur once there is a need for cover-up. Paranoia can take over when attempts to cover up past misdeeds fail. This dynamic was revealed in a dream, in which a man seeking to cover up a sexual misdeed is at risk of being seen and thus thwarted in his cover-up by an innocent bystander; in a moment of irrational desperation, paranoia, and misjudgment, he murders the innocent bystander. A sexual misdeed, followed by failed cover-up, escalates into murder. Each new act of deception generates a new burden of paranoia and delusion for the soul treading down the path of soullessness.

An example of soullessness in the other was conveyed to me by a friend, who had worked as director of religious education at a church. The priest was an alcoholic who was personable and friendly but also abusive; he had previously been demoted from a high level diocesan position. After mass on Sunday, he would inappropriately kiss the women on the lips. In a disagreement with the former religious education director, he had pushed her up against the wall. The situation became so extreme that eight professional staff members of the ministerial team at the church wrote a joint letter to the bishop asking for his intervention. The bishop refused to get involved or to deal with the abuse and alcoholism, instead putting the situation back on the staff, telling them they would need to work with the priest. The staff obtained the assistance of a psychologist who had been a Jesuit, but the therapist didn't address the issue of addiction and abuse. Subsequently, feminists on staff were targeted for the problems in the organization. The director of religious education and liturgist left their jobs; in fact, there was a steady stream of people leaving their jobs. The director of religious education not only left her job but the church as well. Yet for some, the bishop's betrayal

> **Soul carries an inherent largesse, a capacity for ingesting and metabolizing the full range of life's experiences, even difficult and horrific ones, and for creating something of beauty even from the messiness, disappointments, and tragedies of life.**

organic release occurs. This can require a great deal of disciplined attention, for numbness relaxes on its own time table, when it is fully met by awareness. It is as if the density of numbness must be encountered by the spaciousness of awareness, until a quickening happens in the field between them. Then the flow of psychic life to that sector of the body that was formerly numb can be restored. To engage at such a level, with the primal forces of expansion and contraction in the body, puts one in touch with the elemental forces that sustain the universe. It is a numinous experience.

Soullessness in the Other

Encountering soullessness in the other is an entirely different phenomenon from encountering soullessness in oneself, because usually what one encounters are the outer layers of soullessness—the defensive stances, behavioral acts and deception that can accompany soullessness. It is a rather

what one generally encounters in the other are the defensive behavioral manifestations of soullessness, its outer rings. These are the heartless acts committed in everyday life. When this heartlessness moves into calculated strategies to deny "the significance of the other's being," then soullessness moves into outright evil.[12] To align with and enact one's numbness is to identify with soullessness.

To identify with one's evil acts produces additional layers of defensiveness and distancing; shame can turn into shamelessness, where overt false pride in committing shameful acts takes over. Shamelessness and deception then become layered on top of evil behavior, adding extra coating to soullessness. Each new act of evil can produce another layer of shamelessness and deception. The defensive barrier against the sensitivities of the soul, in oneself and others, thickens, with distortions of perception accruing. The shamelessness of the church staff brought about a turning point of seeing evil.

Encounters with evil in the other can evoke a profound shattering within the soul, instigating upheaval and major life transitions. They can singlehandedly disrupt the entire meaning structure of one's life.

To be on the receiving end of another's identification with any of the layers of soullessness is a truly frightening experience. It gives a chill to the whole of one's being, and casts a pall of doubt over the very meaning of existence. To encounter soullessness in another is to question soulfulness in oneself; and by extension, to distrust the principle of soul running through the web of life. So profound is the challenge that witnessing soullessness in another unleashes; it can bring us to stillness, silence, grief, despair. It rocks our very being, sending shockwaves throughout our existence, shattering our foundations, ripping us from the zone of familiar attachments, rupturing the instinctual desire to be in life, altering the soul forever.

When speaking of evil, there is merit in differentiating systemic evil from interpersonal evil. We all live with systemic evil as a daily reality; it is so pervasive as to be normalized and go unrecognized, especially if one lives on the privileged side of this equation, if one is a member of a non-target group. Our economic system, our racial history and structures, our gender arrangements, institutionalize and enshrine oppressive social structures. Oppression is a form of systemic evil, defined by Erica Sherover Marcuse as: "the systemic routine, day-to-day, pervasive, institutionalized mistreatment of a group of people for no other reason than that they are members of that group" (1986, p. 43). Oppressive structures are the externalization of numbness and are fundamentally de-humanizing; they systematically deny, distort and demonize the significance of the other's being.

Along with systemic evil, the interpersonal encounter with evil is deeply disturbing to the soul, because evil now has a human face. When the encounter with evil moves from being impersonal to interpersonal, the soul is profoundly challenged to metabolize the experience. This has to do with the way that the soul metabolizes experience through the personal dimension, through personifying. The process of metabolizing a personal encounter with evil becomes even more challenging when one knows the person and admires or loves the individual for certain other characteristics and qualities.

Because the soul comes to knowledge through personifying dynamics, an interpersonal encounter with evil is particularly chilling and stilling. The consequences of evil may be far greater when transmitted impersonally through systemic processes of oppression. Yet when abusive power dynamics are enacted interpersonally, rather than perpetuated and delivered through an impersonal system of injustice, evil becomes personal, presenting an all too human face. When the transmission is personal, the soul is directly confronted with the raw face of evil.

The human face of evil creates a particular burden for the soul on the receiving end. Evil acts, based in numb hearts, deny the passionate nature of the soul, from whence all meaning in life is ultimately derived. Hence the awake soul that encounters the soullessness of the other is cast into states of meaninglessness and despair. The temptation is

The soul balks at coercion, at distorted or abusive uses of power, and at silencing of its expressive nature.

go asleep precisely at this moment. William Stafford names this tension poetically: "For it is important that awake people be awake.... the darkness around us is deep" (1993, p. 135).

Witnessing the capacity for evil in the other can evoke shock and disbelief, which then grow into confusion, meaninglessness and despair. The taint of evil is so disorienting to normal perception it can temporarily obscure the ability to perceive beauty. I recall one morning awaking from a dream in which I was unable to perceive the beauty in nature, something I knew so well. In order to reaffirm to my senses the reality of beauty, and re-anchor myself in the ability to perceive beauty, I spent that morning gazing at spring flowers blooming in a basket, attempting to portray their delicacy through paint on canvas.

One natural initial response to evil in the other is denial. We do not want to see or believe that this person could be so bad. We still want to belong to this person, to this community that has gone sour yet meant so much to us in the past. But if, from a desire to think well of the other, or to belong to the other, or to think well of the community, or to belong to the community, we deny evil that is really there, the soul will suffer the consequences of this denial and self-deception. If one persists in denial due to the desire to belong despite the presence of evil, one must go numb, enter into soullessness, and begin to collude with evil. One must lose contact with the feeling parts of oneself, sacrificing some of the soul's sensitivities. Evil is like a vortex that sucks people into its force field; at a certain point, one is either pulled further into the vortex, or one must take a stand and eject oneself from it.

Pseudo-innocence is Rollo May's term for the adult's retreat into childhood naivete, an adult fixation on childhood never outgrown. Facing issues too big and too horrendous to contemplate, we "shrink into this kind of innocence and make a virtue of powerlessness, weakness and helplessness. It is this innocence that cannot come to terms with the destructiveness in one's self or others, and hence... it actually becomes self destructive. Innocence that cannot include the daimonic becomes evil" (May, 1972, p. 49-50).

It is possible to collude in the dynamics of evil, even though one did not intend to commit evil. The longer a person lives within a field of evil, the more likely it is that one will begin to collude with evil, carrying out actions on behalf of the evil field. Often within a field of evil, there is a figure who is leading in the evildoing; this figure may engage in acts of intimidation, interrogation, and humiliation, in order to enlist collusion of members of the group. The control of information and interpretation are necessary to maintain this closed system. Those invested in maintaining the closed system will use their power to enforce their interpretations and define the interactions and rules of the system.

Evil requires a higher purpose to justify and cover its actions. Each evil action will require justification on the basis of some higher principle. This higher justification for lower deeds creates an additional layer of confusion for those caught within a field of evil. It is one aspect of the fog of confusion that must be sorted out in liberating oneself from an evil system.

A fog of confusion about what is me and what is the other can reign over the field of evil. When one is inside a field of evil, the entire field can become delusional, due to the intentional deception and paranoia being sown into the field by the evil one(s). The intense distrust and reality distortion of the evildoer infects the entire field. Anyone in that field can be contaminated with the paranoia and deception that is disowned and projected outward by the evildoer.

The direct encounter with evil takes one to a place that very few travel willingly or consciously. People lash out against evil, and try to move away from it, and those are natural responses. Indeed, it is necessary to preserve oneself in the face of evil, or at least attempt to do so, with all the fortitude of one's being. Otherwise, one risks being destroyed by evil; furthermore the attempt at self-preservation in the face of evil is necessary to retain one's most precious asset, dignity.

In addition to self-preservation in the face of evil, it is also important to realize that evil is a place that people sometimes go to—decent, well-intentioned people, the person next door. Fortunately, very few people make a career of evil, but it is still a place that ordinary people dip into. It is a place that people go to when numbness, shame and fear (of discovery of their shameful acts) lead to secrecy, calculated deception, and deceit.

There is an inherently destructive element to evil; for evil constitutes an attack on life, on creation; it is an anti-life force. Yet in the end, evil is destruc-tive to itself. Ultimately evil destroys itself. But it can still destroy ever so much in its wake, before turning inward and destroying itself. The inherently self-destructive trajectory of evil is poignantly portrayed in the film *Downfall*, about the closing days of the Third Reich, when evil turns in upon itself. Of his own suicidal volition, Hitler and his new bride end up "in a ditch covered in petrol, on fire".[13]

Waking Up from Evil

We need to understand objectively the subjective combination of numbness, shame, fear, and calculated deception—to which we give the name evil. And we must understand it as an all too human possibility, and as something that calls out for being related to. Relating to this human possibility means staying in relationship to all that the encounter with evil in the other evokes in oneself –shock, confusion, guilt, self-doubt, disgust, victimization, self-negation, and despair. Consciously enduring this combination of extreme and unpleasant subjective states will surely dismember any construction of self fashioned with lingering holes of pseudo-innocence.

Liberation from the field of evil may require an initial experience of being dumb-struck or struck blind, where the reality of one's one senses, body and deepest knowing suddenly clash with truth of one's inner being that the evil system is covertly subverting.

Comprehending evil as an interpersonal reality requires the soul to feel all the way through how it is affected by being in the presence of the inability to be affected. This is the paradoxical challenge that evil presents.

Initially in working through how I am affected by another person's evil, there is confusion about where the wrongdoing is located; it can feel like I'm wrong or there's something wrong with me. When a person is acting out evil in my direction, I can come to feel that I myself am evil. This sense of something wrong within me relates to the actual fact that somewhere inside me there is an evil part, or the potential for the very same evil. It's not that I don't hold the same potential to enact evil as the other; however, perhaps at this moment, in this situation, it may be that I am not enacting evil, but rather reacting to evil coming in my direction. To believe that the evil or the potential for evil is only over there, in the other person, is to fall into a good-bad split. This psychological splitting becomes the basis for demonizing and scapegoating the other; such scapegoating dynamics are prominent in group and collective life, due to the collective disowning of shadow material.

If one is truly not identified with evil it becomes critical to realize that evildo-

In the encounter with soullessness in the other, authentic power, the power of soul, is being called forth to rise up.

the reality distortion of the evil field. Such a jarring moment may elicit disorienting shock and serve as the beginning of a wake-up call, where one cannot continue to normalize the system while simultaneously maintaining one's sense of self. One cannot live with oneself and continue to go along with the system; something has become intolerable. The body, dreams, people outside the system, people also struggling within the system, can serve to further affirm the ing in this situation originates primarily outside of oneself, and to make the differentiation of locating the enactment of evil in the other, while simultaneously knowing the potential for the same evil within oneself. When one is able to separate and leave the field, it becomes possible to get a reality check, and to differentiate oneself from the taint and distortion of wrongdoing being generated within the field of evil. One can begin to see, 'oh no, it wasn't me enacting that evil, it was that evil field that

I was a part of.' As I work through the dynamics, I come to: 'I'm not doing evil in this situation; the source of evil lives over there, outside of me; I have been reacting to a field of evil, and the evil-doing is sourced primarily in another individual.'

If by chance one is able to become aware of the vulnerable, injured parts that lie hidden behind the evil exterior of the other, it can open a magical doorway to compassion. A key piece of information can help contextualize another person's evil; learning about a secret that stands behind the evildoer's actions can provide relief from the fugue and confusion that evil generates. Gaining distance from the situation and getting help with processing how one is affected by the evil of another assist one with finding the necessary perspective and detachment from evil.

A personal encounter with evil tends to sow seeds of deep distrust in humanity as a whole. Because of this generalized distrust, re-establishing and deepening the bonds of relationship and community with others, especially others who have witnessed firsthand the same evil, and are similarly engaged in a process of waking up from it, can provide vital healing balm to the soul.

Additionally, dreams can pierce the fog of confusion and ground one into what's really going on. People in a field of evil receive dream images related to the distortions and evil enactments, such as images of sleeping with the enemy or images of the evildoer depicted in shocking ways or extreme states. Dream images help provide the necessary reality check; they may exaggerate the situation in order to get one's attention and shock one into painful truths. Both dreaming and waking images that break through consciousness that is still in partial denial about the evil situation assist with realigning with reality.

The encounter with evil in the other will shatter and scatter the fragments of the self to the four directions. But if this fragmenting can be endured consciously, then the self will re-cohere more solid than before. If the self has sufficiently formed and is not destroyed by the encounter, a durable self, a veritable rock of Gibraltar, can emerge from the ash heap. The integrity of the soul and solidity of the self can emerge from the ashes of evil. The encounter with evil in the other forces the issue of one's own integrity. In the economy of the soul, evil in the other either destroys the innocent self, or elicits greater alignment and integrity. If evil has a purpose, this might be it. Ultimately the integrity of the self, my own self, is the only durable thing one can cling to. The integrity of the self is the only thing that cannot be destroyed by this world.

Concerning the process of waking up from numbness, Lifton poignantly writes:

> The vacuum state could, paradoxically, be a prelude to symbolic rebirth. Psychic numbing and despair could serve as a means of 'holding on' prior to taking the first steps toward reintegration. But for this to happen, the patterns of disintegration had to be interrupted—the whole city [the zone of evil], so to speak, had to be 'detoxified.' Only then could three fundamental qualities of active existence within the self-process be reasserted: the sense of connection, the sense of life-energy and movement, and the sense of symbolic integrity or meaning. (Lifton, 1969, p. 90)

To stare awake into the face of evil in the other, and not close one's heart, not join in the numbness, is a test of soul that requires an authentic purification of the self. The evil in the other can become a catalyst for self-purification, but only if that evil is honestly faced and metabolized; only if, at some decisive moment, one dis-identifies from the evil; only if the meaninglessness and despair evoked at being witness to soullessness are tolerated; and only if creative expression and creative action in response to the evil is found. The process of self-purification requires surrender of falsehoods within oneself, a sacrifice of false power and pretense. It is humbling to see the limits of one's own power in the face of the misused power of the other. This humbling and shedding of illusions about one's false power can lead, paradoxically, to a claiming of one's true power.

In the encounter with soullessness in the other, authentic power, the power of soul, is being called forth to rise up. The power of soul lives in the human capacities— courage, fierceness, compassion, autonomy, humility, integrity. The encounter with evil in the other can elicit a deeper immersion in soul and truer inner alignment with self. This encounter calls for surrendering more deeply to the autonomous potency of the life force, as it flows through one's own body and being. Evil can inspire a more perfect love of truth, beauty and justice. This phenomenon is illustrated in the moving stories of holocaust survivors, who engaged their ordeal with evil by becoming ever more human. The encounter with evil can thus serve as an initiatory threshold, in which the soul becomes ever more soulful in response to soullessness.[14]

Soul and Soullessness

Human soullessness is a dense and complex phenomenon. Multiple lenses and interdisciplinary approaches are required to comprehend the phenomenon of soullessness. Theology, philosophy, literature, mythology, sociology, biology, art, and psychology each have contributions to make to our shared understanding of soullessness. All of the psychological orientations have something to enrich the discourse on soullessness and evil. However, in the end, those perspectives that provide the most versatility, range, complexity and depth may offer the most to the conversation on evil.

Imaginal psychology's inherent interest in the range of subjective states,

To stare awake into the face of evil in the other, and not close one's heart, not join in the numbness, is a test of soul that requires an authentic purification of the self.

together with its understanding that all subjective states ultimately belong to the life of the soul, provide an embracing and humane standpoint for facing and engaging the multi-faceted phenomena of soullessness and evil. Perhaps the ability to handle a difficult and dense subject such as human evil presents a test-case for imaginal psychology. In the end, the power of imagery, the language of soul, and a penchant for probing into the range and extremity of subjective states may impart the greatest gifts for understanding the unfathomable.

The imagery of a multi-faceted crystal and a black hole both come to mind in contemplating the task of bringing objectivity to the subjectivity of evil: the crystal because of the complexity inherent in its many facets and transparency through which light passes; the black hole because of its impenetrable dark depths. What both images have in common is density; the black hole exists in a state of utmost density; while the crystal is forged through enduring the pressure of dense forces. The black hole, which engulfs light, the light of consciousness, offers an image of untransmuted soullessness. The crystal, emerging from the pressure of dense forces, passes light through it, refracting light into a rainbow of color, suggesting the process of transmuting the density of soullessness into lucid perception.

Notes

[1] Aftab Omer and Melissa Schwartz are co-founders of the Institute of Imaginal Studies, now known as Meridian University, in Petaluma, California, where the newly coalescing orientation of imaginal psychology has an academic home. See http://www.MeridianUniversity.edu.

[2] While in colloquial speech religion and religious have come to refer to the established religious traditions, and spiritual to the more personal, experiential aspect of religion, here religious is used in the old etymological sense. The origins of Latin religio derive from the same root as ligament, ligare, meaning "bind, connect"; thus, re-ligare, i.e. re (again) + ligare or "to reconnect."

[3] The "river of imagination" is Omer's term.

[4] Imaginal Transformation Praxis (ITP) consists of concepts, principles, and practices that constitute an integrative approach to personal and cultural transformation. ITP has three distinct components: 1.Imaginal Process: an approach to transformative learning, understood as the emergence and cultivation of capacities by individuals, organizations, communities, and societies. 2. Imaginal Inquiry: a methodology for participatory research that weaves together both inquiry and transformation. 3. Cultural Leadership Praxis: a creative and collaborative approach to fostering cultural transformation within organizations, communities, and societies (Omer, 2008).

[5] Aftab Omer referred to dreams as "maps of the soul's unfolding." (Personal communication, October 2006).

[6] Anne Coelho assisted in clarifying how an imbalance among the passions can also be an expression of soullessness. An example of attending to certain passions while neglecting others is being caught up with a passion for cocaine while neglecting one's children and other parts of life. Another example might be someone who attends to their own desire but neglects justice. This kind of imbalance, associated with an over-identification with certain passions, with being consumed by a single passion, with addiction and with an addictive nature, is another form of soullessness.

[7] Jung credits Pierre Janet for our knowledge of the extreme dissociability of consciousness, in which "each fragment of personality has its own peculiar character and its own separate memory. These fragments subsist relatively independently of one another and can take one another's place at any time, which means that each fragment possesses a high degree of autonomy, [giving a] disquieting picture of the possibilities of psychic disintegration" (The Essential Jung, ed. Anthony Storr, 1983, p. 39).

[8] For a fuller discussion of mind control theory, see http://en.wikipedia.org/wiki/Mind_control. Accessed 2/24/09.

[9] Anne Coelho suggested the valuable clarifications in this paragraph about the role of symptoms in the life of the soul.

[10] Anne Coelho assisted me with teasing apart the ideas that appear in this section, offering valuable clarifications about numbness as an expression of the soul's tendency to create symptoms, and about the possibility of numbness being passionately defended and enacted.

[11] In traditional symbolism, the crocodile carries four types of symbolic meaning (Cirlot, 1991). First, because of its perceived vicious and destructive power, the crocodile came to signify fury and evil in Egyptian hieroglyphics. Second, since it inhabits an intermediate realm between earth and water, where it is associated with mud and vegetation, it became an emblem of fecundity and power. Third, it is associated with the symbols of inversion and rebirth. A fourth aspect relates to the dragon and the serpent, guardians of treasures and symbolic of hidden wisdom. Crocodiles bring opportunities to touch very primal energies, as well as the opportunity for birth and initiation, signaling the culmination of knowledge on one level and an opening to new knowledge and wisdom (Andrews, 2001, p. 354-355).

[12] The phrase "to maintain the significance of the other's being" comes from Aftab Omer's definition of a culture of conviviality. (2008, November 18). Concepts from Imaginal Transformation Theory, Petaluma, CA.

[13] This is Eddie Izzard's expression.

[14] I wish to express my gratitude to all those who reviewed and commented upon earlier versions of this article: Anne Coelho, Jurgen Kremer, Kimmy Johnson, Lisa Herman, and Isoke Femi. These insightful readers have assisted me with a number of refinements that have added complexity and richness to my own thinking about the phenomenon of soul and soullessness.

References

Aizenstat, S. (2009). *Dream-tending*. New Orleans, LA: Spring Journal Books.

Andrews, T. (2001). *Animal-speak: The spiritual and magical powers of creatures great and small*. St. Paul, MN: Llewellyn Publications.

Cirlot, J.E. (1991). *A dictionary of symbols*. New York: Dorset Press.

Edinger, E. (1974). *Ego and archetype: Individuation and the religious function of the psyche*. Baltimore, MD: Penguin Books.

Hillman, J. (1992). *Re-visioning psychology*. New York: HarperPerennial.

Lakoff, G. and Johnson, M. (1980). *Metaphors we live by*. Chicago: University of Chicago Press.

Levine, P. (1997). *Waking the tiger: Healing trauma*. Berkeley, CA: North Atlantic Books.

Lifton, R. J. (1969). *Death in life: Survivors of Hiroshima*. New York: Vintage Books, 1969.

May, R. (1972). *Power and innocence: A search for the sources of violence*. New York: W.W. Norton & Co.

Miller, A. (1986). *For your own good: Hidden cruelty in child-rearing and the roots of violence*. Toronto: Collins Publishers

Moore, T. (1994). *Care of the soul: A guide for cultivating depth and sacredness in everyday life*. New York: HarperPerennial.

Nathanson, D. L. (1992). *Shame and pride: Affect sex and the birth of the self*. New York: W.W Norton & Company.

Omer A. (2003, July 14). Imaginal psychology in context. Lecture given at Institute of Imaginal Studies, Petaluma, CA.

Omer, A. (2008, November 18). Concepts from imaginal transformation praxis. Petaluma CA.

Omer, A & Kremer J. (2003). Between Columbine and the twin towers. *ReVision*, 26(2), 37-40.

Peck, S. (1983). *The people of the lie: The hope for healing human evil*. New York: Touchstone.

Peck, S. (2003). *The road less traveled: A new psychology of love, traditional values and spiritual growth*. New York: Touchstone.

Sherover-Marcuse, E. (1986). *Emancipation and consciousness*. Oxford: Blackwell Publishers

Stafford, W. (1993). *The darkness around us is deep: Selected poems of William Stafford*. New York: HarperPerennial.

Storr, A. (Ed.) (1983). *The essential Jung*. New York: MJF Books.

The Shadow of the American Dream:

The Clash of Class Ascension and Shame

Helen Joy Policar

The American dream and the struggles of the working class have been widely discussed and analyzed leading up to the presidential election in 2008. Barack Obama has been held up as a beacon of hope for those struggling to achieve the American dream. In January of 2008, Obama delivered a campaign speech in Kansas in which he declares that his belief in and realization of the American dream has been the foundation of his success. He describes his maternal grandparents as working class people who suffered hardship during the depression, but believed through hard work and determination they could provide a better life for their children:

> My grandparents held on to a simple dream—that they could raise my mother in a land of boundless opportunity; and that their generation's struggle and sacrifice could give her the freedom to be what

Joy Policar, Ph.D. is a psychologist in private practice in Davis, California and presents workshops on social class for educators and psychotherapists. Her work with clients is influenced by her first career as a high school English teacher and guidance counselor. Her eclectic approach awakens imagination resulting in a more authentic and multi-faceted self image. Her workshops engage the profound impact of social class identity in education and psychotherapy. Joy is a graduate of the Institute of Imaginal Studies; her dissertation, upon which this article is based, is entitled "Class Identity: The Experience of Shame in Realizing the American Dream."

she wanted to be; to live how she wanted to live. (Obama, 2008, p. 2)

He goes on to say, "The dream we share is more powerful than the differences we have—because I am living proof of that ideal"(p. 3).

Although Obama's speech, "Reclaiming the American Dream," is emotionally stirring and his rise up the class ladder is admirable, it fails to reveal or comment on the underlying assumptions of the American Dream that are linked to class identity shame. Within the myth of the American Dream, moving up the social class ladder, for instance growing up as a member of the working class in which neither parent has a college education and subsequently achieving professional middle class status through education, much like Obama's family story, is seen not only as unquestionably desirable; but is also perceived as equally accessible to all and bringing ultimate satisfaction. However, the idealized version of the American dream that is often portrayed in American literature, film, and television, does not address that members of the working class often carry feelings of deep shame and inferiority that are not ameliorated through class ascension.

The nuances of shame that relate to class identity, create internal conflict and struggle, states of inner tension that can only be resolved and transformed

through acknowledging and experientially turning toward this powerful affect. Turning towards the potent inhibiting affect of shame requires the safety of a contained space in which the vulnerabilities associated with shame may be touched and transmuted. Thus, those who work most closely with the subjective states associated with class identity, including psychologists and educators, are compelled not only to be aware of the cultural taboos against discussing class identity and shame, but also equipped to provide emotionally safe containers that facilitate breaking through the defensive posturing that often covers class shame. Only within such a safe space can shame be consciously experienced and transformed into something more, the dignity, integrity and autonomy of true selfhood.

Links Between Class Identity, Shame, and the American Dream

Paul Fussell (1983) and others who have researched class identity in American culture find that America is a highly stratified society in which the professional middle and upper classes enjoy a myriad of unearned tangible and intangible privileges, such as personal contacts with employers, good childhood health care, and superior educational opportunities to name a few, at the expense of those in subordinate classes (Ohman 2003; Linkon 1999). The literature also reveals that American television and film often portray those in lower and working classes as less intelligent, attractive, and capable than their counterparts in dominant classes (Scharrer 2001; Ehrenreich 1989; Butsch 2003).

Noticing and speaking about these class distinctions is taboo in American culture. Although reluctant to discuss inequitable social class privileges, Americans are divided along class lines by a rigid set of external standards that contribute to the formation of class identity (Fussell 1983). Class identity is based upon multiple factors, such as outer appearances, status of family of origin, interests, tastes, education, mannerisms, speech patterns, professional status, income level, and material possessions to name a few. Although not as overtly identifiable as race or gender, identification with a social class constitutes an integral part of personal identity.

Kaufman posits (1992, pp. 78-79) that people develop their identities through positive and negative identifications. One's sense of belonging is developed through identification with a group. Class identity is formed through the association one makes with others that form a group comprised of a particular social class. Kaufman (80) asserts that the majority culture will impose negative images on any minority group. Members of minority groups internalize these negative images, which result in shame-laden conflicted identities. Although members of the working class are not in a minority in America, they often perceive themselves in a less desirable position than those of the professional middle class and above. Freire's (1970, 59) conception of internalized oppression assists in understanding the cultural negativity and animosity toward the working class. He states that the oppressed class often internalizes their oppressors' opinions of them, which reinforces the inequities of class stratification.

Numerous studies indicate that working-class people often experience shame based on their subordinate and devalued position in the social hierarchy. For example, Richard Sennett and Jonathan Cobb's (1972) seminal research reveals that working-class men blame themselves for their inferior social position. Furthermore, the literature reveals (Law, 1985; Tokarczyk & Fay, 1993; Grimes & Morris, 1997) that ascending into the professional middle class does not ameliorate the identity conflicts and

The idealized version of the American dream that is often portrayed in American literature, film, and television, does not address that members of the working class often carry feelings of deep shame and inferiority that are not ameliorated through class ascension.

emotional pain of working-class people. Although shame has not been the focus of the previously mentioned literature, this painful affect is important to more fully explore as it may be at the root of class identity conflicts.

Jeremy Rifkin (2004) and others maintain that the American dream is an integral part of the national collective consciousness. Jennifer Hochschild, (1992) Jim Cullen, (2003) and bell hooks (2000) contend that the American dream assumes that upward mobility is accessible to everyone and can be achieved through individual efforts of hard work, tenacity, and strength of will. According to the American dream, those in lower or working classes who do not attain the enhanced class status and material wealth connected to achievement of this dream are unsuccessful because of their own weaknesses and character flaws (Rifkin 2004). Cullen (2003) makes the point that the tenets of American Dream

have their roots in the Declaration of Independence and are embedded in the national psyche, and contribute to fostering a belief that this nation is superior to all others.

Gershen Kaufman and Lev Raphael (1996) contend that when members of a minority group internalize the dominant culture's negative evaluations of their group, they are at risk for developing a shame-prone identity. Donald Nathanson (1992) explains that the pain of feeling shame is so intolerable, people develop a set of maladaptive defenses in order to avoid it. Andrew Morrison's (1996) remarks about shame reflect the work of numerous others who have studied this affect. He says:

Shame is a feeling of self-castigation that arises when we are convinced that there is something about ourselves that is wrong, inferior, flawed, weak or dirty. Shame is fundamentally a feeling of loathing against ourselves, a hateful vision of ourselves through our own eyes—although this vision may be determined by how we expect other people are experiencing us. (p. 13)

Thomas Scheff (2003) espouses that strong taboos exist in American culture surrounding social class and shame. The idea that American class divisions result in oppression, and the notion that in spite of hard work and talent people may not achieve upward mobility, contradict the assumptions of the American dream (hooks 2000). Since individuals are held personally and even at times morally responsible for their position on the class ladder, often the psychological conflicts associated with class identity are kept hidden. In addition, when people feel ashamed they desire invisibility, so shame is by nature secretive and hidden (Kaufman 1989). Aftab Omer (2001) and others posit that in order to transform shame, it must be fully acknowledged and experienced (Scheff 2003; Kaufman & Raphael 1996; Nathanson 1992).[1]

Because the affect of shame is so excruciatingly painful to bring into awareness, humans have developed a series of defenses against shame, which Nathanson calls "the compass of shame" (Nathanson, 1992, pp. 310-313). These styles of defense are separated into four poles which are: withdrawal, avoidance, attack-self, and attack-other. The withdrawal defensive strategy is characterized by a moving away or withdrawing from the painful feelings that a shame experience evokes. Withdrawal happens rapidly while avoidance is a slow and deliberate process of moving away. Avoidance is characterized by a hiding of the inner self and involves donning false personas. There is an attempt to fool others by presenting a false self that is perceived to be pleasing to them. The attack-self and attack-other defensive strategies are connected to relationships with others. Attack-self comes in the form of deference to another through shyness, self-deprecation, and conformity, and at the far end of the pole, masochism. Attack-other is characterized by a bolstering of self-esteem through the denigration of another.

Upward Mobility: A Personal Experience of Class Shame

Journeying through the nine-year process of earning a doctoral degree and becoming a licensed psychologist, I have had the opportunity to recognize and acknowledge my class identity shame. The experiential work, the process of conducting the research, and writing a dissertation on class identity brought to the surface how deeply I had experienced feelings of shame and inadequacy most of my life. My graduate training assisted me in acknowledging my shame, feeling it, and understanding the defenses I often use to deflect it. My dissertation research gave me the opportunity to provide a container in which others who had class issues similar to my own were able to face their shame and shift toward its transmutation. As I studied class identity shame and the defenses people use to mitigate its sting, I personally underwent a process of healing some of the wounds of

my own class shame. In another words, I lived the topic I was studying.

I emerged from this process with a much better understanding of how and why I have attempted to cover up feelings of inadequacy by inflating my

Photo: Astrid Berg, www.astridberg.com

accomplishments, imitating the tastes of the upper classes, disparaging others, and placing undue emphasis on societal measures of success. Drawn to this research topic because of an interest in exploring shame and its relationship to class identity, I wondered about the impact of class identity and shame on others who have had a similar journey to mine. Since the American dream influenced my decisions to move out of the working class, I felt compelled to explore how it had affected others with similar backgrounds. Since I was in my mid-40s before beginning to confront feelings about class identity, my curiosity was sparked about the internal

Turning towards the potent inhibiting affect of shame requires the safety of a contained space in which the vulnerabilities associated with shame may be touched and transmuted.

defensive strategies that are employed to keep this experience at bay and the impact that cultural values have in reinforcing those defenses.

My background is riddled with events in which class shame was operating unconsciously, leaving me confused and unable to understand its destructive impact. When I began the journey toward the dissertation, I had already climbed several rungs up the class ladder, but feelings of shame continued to plague me. I was born into a working class family. My father was a fireman, and my mother was a bank teller and homemaker. My mother did not attend college, and my father was a high school dropout. While I was no longer considered part of the working class, identifying with upper or professional middle-class people filled me with shame and uneasiness. No one in my immediate or extended family on either side had obtained a college degree until I graduated with my Bachelors of Arts at 22. In my mid-20s I earned a single subject teaching credential and ten years later earned a Master of Science degree, along with a Pupil Personnel Services Credential. My 17-year career as a teacher and counselor brought numerous accolades.

Along with professional success, I had ascended to an upper-middle-class lifestyle through marrying an accomplished corporate attorney. Although our spacious home and vacation home exceeded any standard of living I could have imagined possible, I continued to be plagued by feelings of inferiority and shame. While achieving the American dream, I had spent my life trying to break free from the constraints of my background. My desire to move up the social class ladder had been realized, yet this apparent success had not eased the shame and conflict that surrounded my class identity.

When I was growing up, my family did not socialize with professional people with college educations. The only adults I knew with professional status were my medical doctor and my teachers. I did not take any college preparatory classes in high school, as my parents expected me to become an airline stewardess or secretary until I got married. My parents were overwhelmed with financial and personal problems, leaving them unable to monitor the teenage activities of their children. Consequently, my secondary education was a blur of truancy, parties, below-average grades, and boys.

When I began working at a neighborhood department store and befriended people with college interests, I became self-conscious of my family's working class status. At that time, I began dating a young man from work who came from a professional upper middle class family and was attending the local university. He encouraged me to enroll in junior college since my high school graduation was rapidly approaching and I had no post-secondary plans. I did not have academic preparation to enter even a junior college. In fact, I had not read a book or written an essay throughout my secondary education; nor did I have any knowledge of college entrance exams. In the mid-seventies in California there were no entrance or placement exams for junior college, leaving me free to select courses of my choosing without considering the skills that

coursework were formed along class lines. Students were placed in or chose high school courses based on college aspirations and standardized test scores. As a result, my non-college preparatory courses were filled with students whose families had little idea of university entrance requirements. In this new setting I was no longer surrounded by friends.

The instructor's first statement was, "Welcome, you are now part of the educated elite, and I hope you are all qualified to be here." Immediately, color rose to my cheeks; my mind flooded with the reasons that deemed me unqualified. I knew others had taken college preparatory classes, and no one else looked nervous. My insides quivered with fear. What right did I have to be in college?

I heard little of the instructor's course description, but terms and phrases such as rhetoric, classification and division essay, comparison and contrast, and expository writing filled me with a sense of shame and inferiority. For the first time in my life, I experienced the jolt of my difference and felt consciously ashamed of my social position. This included shame of my family, history, academic choices, and myself. Then the teacher instructed us to provide her with a sample of our writing and gave us the

In spite of this proud story of educational achievement, the academic climb to the university broadened the gap between my family of origin and myself. When I told my parents I was going to major in humanities, they had never heard of such a course of study. Although they are intelligent people, they had never been exposed to the history of art and ideas and did not understand the value of an education in the liberal arts. They viewed college as a vehicle to obtaining a job. Hard pressed to explain my fascination with ideas that ranged from Greek humanism to the influences of early Christianity on modern day American life to Renaissance artists, I kept silent and the gulf between us widened. Also I was ashamed of my parents who had such large gaps in the understanding of Western culture which stood in such stark contrast to the university professors I was so enamored with. Conflicted feelings abounded, as I was ashamed of my own feelings of snobbery toward my parents.

At the university, I struggled to fit in with my peers. Some of my classmates from a Shakespearian Tragedy course were at a coffee house discussing a poetry reading they had attended the prior evening. When one of them asked me about my favorite poets, I again, felt the shame rise. Attending a poetry reading on campus was impossible because I worked nearly full time to support myself. I had not yet studied poetry in my college courses and did not have time to read for pleasure or enrichment. Not feeling safe to explain my plight to the group, I feigned remembering leaving a book in the classroom, and hurried off—knowing I would never be one of them.

Although I did not engage in the university social life, I was successful academically. Graduating with a Bachelor of Arts in English and Humanities, and later attending the University of California and earning a teaching credential, I built a successful career as a high school English teacher, often teaching honors and advanced placement literature courses. Yet, feelings of inferiority often plagued me when teaching intellectually gifted students from professional middle-class families.

In my personal life, feelings of infe

Related to cultural taboos around class and shame in America, outward public behaviors offer no hint to the private intensity of shame and inferiority scripts that surround working-class identity.

might be needed. In retrospect, it seems my elementary education provided me enough of a foundation in reading and math in order to achieve my subsequent academic success.

Entering junior college, I enrolled in lower division courses, including college English Composition, which I had first period, the first day of school. As we filed into the room, I noticed some of my former high school classmates who were from wealthier neighborhoods. At our high school, groups and

last 25 minutes of the period to work. I could not recall sustaining thinking for 25 minutes on any one topic, let alone compose a piece of writing—yet somehow I was able to complete the task.

Although I struggled through my courses, I eventually mastered skills needed to succeed academically and earned an Associate Degree. I transferred to the local state university where my sense of displacement, doubt of my qualifications, and shame about my history lingered.

riority regarding class identity surfaced dramatically when I married a professional upper-middle-class man. I was conscious of the fact that I was marrying someone who did not share my class background. While his parents financed his college and graduate school studies, I had financed my education by working as a sales clerk and, later, a manager in the retail clothing business. Since we were in our mid- to late-30s when we married, both of us were established in our professional lives. When we were planning our wedding, I was apprehensive about bringing our two families together. Both of my brothers have had serious drug addictions. My younger brother had been stealing jewelry and appliances from our mother's home. I was worried he might steal from our guests or cause a scene, since his behavior was so erratic.

To ease my anxiety, I hired an undercover security guard with specific instructions to watch my younger brother closely and physically remove him if the need arose. My fiancé had difficulty imagining what might occur and was puzzled about my decision. Not only was I concerned about my brother's emotional state and behavior, I was also anxious about several of my cousins who had a myriad of emotional problems, criminal records, and lack of skills to meet their survival needs. Oddly, the wedding took place without incident; however, my nervousness about what might occur mirrored the reality of the differences between these two families. My husband's older brother is a renowned gynecologist, while my older brother had been working at Rainbow Bread factory, operating a bread-slicing machine, for over 15 years.

Later, I earned a Master of Science degree in educational counseling while teaching full time, and then secured a position as high school guidance counselor. The voices of shame and inferiority often played loudly in my head when I met with professional parents about college opportunities for their children. With 500 students in my caseload, I counseled students with a range of abilities and differing levels of achievement. It was difficult to feel worthy enough to counsel high-achieving honors students that were headed for the most elite universities in the country.

In addition, I have felt conflicted regarding my upper-middle-class social status. My husband is Jewish, and while preparing for my son's Bar Mitzvah, my class issues rose to the surface. My husband and his family took for granted that this coming of age ceremony would also include an extravagant celebration. Conflicted about planning such an event, I took every opportunity to relay to the party decorators and disc

Avoidant defenses, such as denial, intellectualizing, humor, and superiority stances, serve to mask class identity shame.

jockeys that things were going "over the top." I joked with them about people who I imagined felt no compunction about spending thousands of dollars on a party, trying to make sure they understood my working-class roots. Ashamed about my conspicuous consumption, I was certain that the party helpers viewed me negatively.

Although I enjoyed my doctoral coursework, my class identity shame continued to grip me, as I struggled with feeling inferior intellectually and academically to my classmates. The experiential activities in the courses fostering self-awareness provided the first opportunity for me to acknowledge that I was defending against class identity shame, but it was the dissertation process that assisted me in the transformational process. The research was designed to evoke the experience of class shame and explore both the defenses against shame and the inner experiences of the participants. Activities at the meetings were designed so that participants underwent experiences of class shame and reacted to them. In other words, the data was gleaned from fresh experiences rather than descrip-

tions or recounting of feelings that may have taken place in the past.

Experiences of shame associated with class identity shame were evoked through viewing film clips, participating in an activity that generated memories related to the shadow of growing up in the working class, listening to songs that exemplify cultural attitudes about class ascension, and participating in a role play that explored cultural biases about the working class. Participants expressed their experience by journal writing, painting, and group discussion. Journal writings were the primary mode of data collection, and several discussions in which participants responded to activities were audiotaped and transcribed.

I engaged in a parallel process with my participants during research meetings and the subsequent interpretive sessions with my research assistant, using every shred of my defensive armor to deflect shame. As participants built walls of avoidance and denial, I built towers. Like the participants, I was unaware that I wore a heavy suit of defensive armor. When I was unable to tolerate the intensity of my shame, I privately attacked the credibility of the process and my participants. When participants reacted to experiences differently than expected, I dove head first into a dark pool of self-loathing, anger, fear, and shame. As participants revealed inferiority scripts, my sense of unworthiness intensified. This arduous process left me confused, and, at several junctures, I lost faith in my research and ability. However, as I witnessed the participants' shifts toward authentic experience, my defensive structures began to break down, giving rise to new insights in my turn toward self-reflection.

Psychological Components of Class Identity Shame

My doctoral research on the relationship of class identity and shame explored psychological aspects of class identity shame. The study was conducted within the participatory paradigm using a distinct methodology, Imaginal

Inquiry, which has four phases: evoking, expressing, interpreting, and integrating experience. This methodology calls for participants to directly experience the subject being researched. Since validity in the participatory paradigm is based on authenticity, it was important that participants directly experience shame related to class identity during the research meetings. In order to evoke experience, activities were planned to urge participants to step out of their normative identities, rather than merely reminiscing about shame experiences related to class. Participants attended three three-hour group meetings, in which they confronted a number of intense experiences related to class shame. The five primary learnings from my research are summarized below.

First, my research showed that related to cultural taboos around class and shame in America, outward public behaviors offer no hint to the private intensity of shame and inferiority scripts that surround working-class identity (Policar, 2006). Hochschild (1992), hooks (2000), and Zandy (1995) assert that class is a taboo subject in the United States. They are in agreement that social class—its existence and its effects on citizens—is not at the forefront of the American consciousness. They state that Americans are influenced by a myth of a classless society and blame themselves when they find themselves on the lower rungs of the class ladder. Nathanson (1993) posits that when shame is triggered the inferiority scripts that emerge are characterized by the following themes and feelings: weakness and incompetence; helplessness and dependence; loser in competition; uniqueness rests on defectiveness; personal unattractiveness; sexually inadequate; wishes to be invisible based on fear of exposure; and being unworthy of love.

Helen Block Lewis (1971) theorizes that one of the three types of shame is

bypassed shame. Instead of feeling the shame, it is defended against with the activation of inferiority scripts and feelings of hostility towards others. Several studies point to the negative ways in which working-class people often view themselves. Sennett and Cobb (1972) conclude that the working-class men in their study were ashamed of their educational level, tastes, and economic status. The working-class men they interviewed revealed that they wanted their children to have a better life, which meant ascension from the working class. Lareau (2003) points out that professional middle-class children have opportunities to cultivate talents, opinions, and skills—which all have significant value in this culture.

Secondly, my research revealed that avoidant defenses, such as denial, intellectualizing, humor, and superiority stances, serve to mask class identity shame. Working-class people who have

When avoidant defenses do not sufficiently ameliorate the painful intensity of class shame, shame spirals into anger, expressed in denigrating attacks on others.

ascended to the professional middle-class often avoid topics of loss, grief, and shame associated with their class backgrounds and experiences (Policar, 2006). Donald Nathanson (1992) contends that avoidant defenses compel

people to lie to themselves or blame others in order to avoid an experience they do not want to feel. Avoidant defenses are characterized by disavowal of experience because of harsh self-assessments and fear of negative evaluation from others. Nathanson (1992, p. 339) says, "We must fool others and fool ourselves." People drawn to avoidance to defend against powerful affect often feel their inner experiences are inferior and if exposed would point to their inadequacy. Therefore, people who defend against shame with avoidance create false selves they think are more acceptable to others. These false selves or artificial personas serve to distract others from the judgment that the true self is defective.

Higher education is often a way for people to ascend from the working class to the professional middle class. The sting of class shame can be mitigated through dodging feelings by engaging the intellect (Policar, 2006). Also the cultural norms of the professional middle class favor intellectualizing over emoting (Demott, 1990). John Bradshaw (1988, p. 105) says, "Intellectualization is often a way to avoid internal states which are shame-bound."

Thirdly, my research demonstrated that when avoidant defenses do not sufficiently ameliorate the painful intensity of class shame, shame spirals into anger expressed in denigrating attacks on others (Policar, 2006). Retzinger (1987) distinguishes between normal rage and shame/rage. She posits that normal rage is characterized as follows: the injury is recognized; it remains conscious; it may be easily resolved; it is not displaced and focuses on an actual cause; and it has few negative results. On the other hand, shame/rage is characterized by feelings of powerlessness: it is denial of the injury; it is pushed from awareness; it creates a circular feeling trap; it is displaced; it becomes a social phenomenon; and it has negative results.

Nathanson (1993) asserts that attack

Photo: Astrid Berg, www.astridberg.com

other defenses are strongly associated with the ways in which people perceive that they compare to others. Primitive concerns dominate these defensive patterns, such as "whether we are large or small, strong or weak, proficient or incompetent, articulate or dumb"(p. 362). According to Nathanson, these feelings become too painful to contain, so people resort to the attack-other defenses, which is characterized by a lashing out of internal feelings at those who have engendered the feelings of powerlessness. Also, when avoidant defenses are no longer easing feelings of inadequacy, attacking others will

their caretakers or by disavowing their own beliefs and desires to align more closely with cultural values. They will then shift the major part of their energies to "the task of molding themselves, by a rigid system of inner dictates, into beings of absolute perfection."(p. 26) People positioned on the lower rungs of the class ladder often are driven to climb the ladder in order to mitigate the pain of feeling less than.

Collective American values and attitudes regarding the working class are internalized by the working class and restrict their experience. Perceptions regarding collective attitudes portrayed

that people with shame-laden identities do not work through the resulting psychological pain unless they expose and confront shame. They state, "The journey toward wholeness must first take us deeper into shame before bringing us out of shame"(p. 14).

Omer proposes that when one turns away from affect, one is unable to develop capacity, which refers to, "A distinct dimension of human evolution and human development that delineates a specific potential for responding to a domain of life experiences."[2] He further suggests that negative affects can be transmuted and developed into capacities. Rather than restricting shame through compensatory defenses, turning toward it can assist in transmuting its negative impact and developing the capacities that result in authentic power. In particular Omer suggests that shame transmutes to autonomy, dignity, and integrity.[3] Omer asserts that when gatekeepers, which are akin to the inner critic, attack the psyche, the authentic self is not able to meet the experience in the present moment. Instead of turning away when shame is triggered, people must develop what Omer terms reflexivity, or self-awareness. To reflexively respond when affect arises requires maintaining a balance between feeling the affect and remaining capable of stepping back from it enough to creatively engage with it. Ways of functioning in the world with reflexivity, he maintains, must be developed and practiced.[4] In order for a person to begin the process of transmutation, a container must be created for these deep affective experiences to come forward.

The internalization of cultural judgments towards the working class and identification with the tenets of the American dream result in conflicted identities for those who ascend from the working class.

usually temporarily help regain feelings of control.

A fourth learning from my research is that the internalization of cultural judgments towards the working class and identification with the tenets of the American dream result in conflicted identities for those who ascend from the working class. Kaufman (1992) states that the inner life is often overwhelmed with competing voices of the self. He explains that people disavow parts of themselves that are too painful to experience. This disowning of different parts of the self results in a conflicted identity in which these parts of the psyche are at war with other parts. Karen Horney (1950) posits that, when living in a competitive culture and "feeling at the bottom," people can develop the need to lift themselves above others. These feelings force one to "override his genuine feelings, wishes, and thoughts, and he is no longer the driver, but is driven."(p. 23) She asserts that, under inner stress, people may become alienated from their real selves. Instead of tending to their needs, they create false selves by adapting to the needs and expectations of

in the media and popular culture toward the working class often include: lack of impulse control, proclivities to anger and violence, tendencies toward substance abuse, lack of ambition, and inferior intelligence. Fred Flinstone, Archie Bunker, Homer Simpson, Dagwood Bumstead, and Rosanne Barr epitomize some of these stereotypes.

A fifth learning from my research showed that emotional containment, safety, and imaginative expression facilitate the acknowledgement and experiencing of class identity shame, along with the shifting of defensive reactions towards self-reflection (Policar 2006). Nathanson (1993) posits that after the first sting of shame, people have a choice as to how they react. He explains that people have physical and emotional responses to shame that are outside their ability to control; however, he contends that we decide whether to defend against unpleasant feelings or accept and learn from them. He says that we can use the trigger of shameful experience as a spur toward personal change.

Kaufman & Raphael (1996) explain

A Personal Transformational Experience

As a result of my graduate education, I have noticed some profound shifts in my identity. The process brought me in contact with the deeper purpose of undertaking this initiatory journey toward a doctoral degree. Although on the surface, earning a doctoral degree represents another way in which to achieve the American dream and distance myself from my working-class roots, the true motivation for taking this journey was buried deep in my unconscious. For several weeks after my dissertation defense, I struggled to make meaning of the process I had undergone. At first I believed that the driving force in my life had been that of conforming to societal standards of success, especially those embedded in the American dream. In the process of completing this dissertation, I came to realize that this compliance is only the conscious part of my journey—it is the surface story that has framed my soul's desires. The deeper journey had been my soul's imperative, nudging me forward into the dark forest and deep uncharted waters to discover more of who I really am. What I thought was a story of class ascension is deeper story of my adaptive identity struggling to discover my soul's desire. Adaptive identity refers to the adaptive patterns of reactivity that the developing soul constellates in the course of coping with environmental impingement, as well as overwhelming events; "these self images persist as an adaptive identity into subsequent contexts where they are maladaptive and barriers to the unfolding of being" (Omer, A. personal communication, April 28, 2006). Striving for upward mobility makes perfect sense to those (myself included) embedded in the cultural trance that prestige, status, and money bring fulfillment. My ego had believed this, but the research process helped me discover that my journey is a soulful one—it was the only journey I could take. Taking the steps of the soul's journey is frightening. Hence, framing my story as one of climbing the social ladder, one aligned with cultural norms, brought comfort. Until nearly the end of the process, the ways in which my wounds have bound me to my past and to my adaptive identity, and held me prisoner, have remained largely unconscious.

Approximately a week after I defended my dissertation I had a disturbing dream. Yet it was that dream that provided insight into my transformational journey and the alchemical process. I live in a large home that is decorated with beautiful paintings and tasteful furniture, and is accessorized with an array of objects of art from blown glass plates to iron sculptures. An elegant four by eight foot original oil painting, portraying a riverbank scene in Sacramento, is the focal point in the family room. This vivid dream depicted my house catching fire and burning to the ground.

In the first image in the dream, I notice smoke escaping from beneath my clothes closet in the master bedroom. When I opened the closet door, my first thought was to retrieve the fine jewelry that was locked in a safe and bolted to the closet shelf. Unable to salvage my clothes already engulfed in

Emotional containment, safety, and imaginative expression facilitate the acknowledgement and experiencing of class identity shame, along with the shifting of defensive reactions towards self-reflection.

flames, I snatched the safe's keys from the dresser drawer, but the keys would not work. Frantic, I began pulling at the safe's handle with all my strength, but it would not budge. I left the pieces of jewelry my husband had given me over the fourteen years of our marriage to burn. I ran out of the house and was relieved to spot my son, husband, and cat in a field across the street from our house. We sat helplessly and watched the house burn to the ground. But to my surprise and delight when I looked over my shoulder, the large painting lay in the weeds undamaged by the fire. My husband had retrieved it from the wall before escaping the flames.

I had been haunted by the significance of this dream and reflected on the meaning of the painting being the only possession salvaged from the fire. This painting, entitled "Crossing Over," is six years old. My husband and I commissioned an artist to create a painting for our home because we were drawn to her landscape pieces previously seen in an art show. The commission was undertaken with the understanding that, if the finished piece did not meet our expectations, we were under no obligation to buy it. The artist and I met a few times in my home to assist her in understanding my expectations. She agreed to paint a landscape, but we did not discuss specifics of the content or composition of the painting. However, in the course of the conversation, I revealed to her that I was raised in a run down, crime-ridden area of South Sacramento near the river.

We did not have much contact during the year in which she created the piece, and it was during that time that I made a decision to leave my work with the school district where I had been employed for seventeen years. The day she informed me that painting was complete was the day I resigned from the school district I had not seen the painting nor discussed it with the artist. I was taken aback when she brought it into my home because it depicted an area near my childhood home, on the Sacramento River—Garcia Bend—where I often hung out with friends as a teenager. Tears filled my eyes because I could not believe a scene so breathtaking could be a part of my childhood experience. It seemed that the painting represented my childhood and old neighborhood, and its title, "Crossing Over," symbolized my class ascension. I thought the meaning of the painting was that I literally crossed over the river into a better life. The bank of the river portrayed in the painting is stunning, but it is the water that has a mesmerizing quality. I did not realize that I had been flailing in that water during the process of finishing graduate school and writing my dissertation.

Hence, the painting has come to mean something much different since have completed my dissertation. In the dream, it survived the fire because it represents my soul's journey. The river in the painting does not represent my crossing over or separation from my roots as I previously thought. The river bank is part of the old neighborhood an belongs in my home because my roots are a part of me. In fact, the represen tation of that riverbank scattered with its ancient cottonwood trees, symbolizes my roots, a part of me that holds unspeakable beauty and strength just as the trees on the riverbank. I did not cross over into a better life—the crossing over is about the identity shift of accepting every part of myself. The riverbank is not the old me—it is me. The crossing of the ethereal river depicted in the painting is my soul's journey into wholeness and self-acceptance.

I believe that the fire in this dream represents the alchemical process that I underwent during my doctoral coursework, and more specifically, the dissertation process. The burning of my clothes represents the transformation of my identity. Clothes are the covering of the body—they cover those aspects of the body not meant for others to see. My protective armoring was burned, but not from my body—it was burned from my psyche.

The defensive structures that I have used to cover my class shame were mirrored for me through the behaviors of the participants. Like them, the inflated intellectual stances and denial that comes with avoidant defenses had been part of my repertoire. Attacking and disparaging others had been my defense of choice to cover the gnawing sense of inferiority that I had felt all of my life. Witnessing the participants attack and disparage others triggered an overwhelming sense of disgust toward them. The process of interpreting the data and understanding my own wounding helped me to see that the disgust I felt toward them was the way in which I felt about myself. The journey toward compassion for the participants opened up compassion for myself. The class identity shame I had experienced in my life was digested and transmuted toward compassion for others as well as myself.

My unsuccessful attempt to salvage the jewelry represents my letting go of the guise of sophistication that has masked my feelings of inferiority. My husband has gifted me with several pieces of fine jewelry including sapphire, diamond, and ruby necklaces, rings, earrings, and bracelets. Over the years, wearing this jewelry has been a way for me to show others that I am part of the upper-middle-class. These

Photo: Astrid Berg

motives have been unconscious, but, upon reflection, I see that donning the jewelry was like wearing a sign that said, "Hey, look at me; I have money and am better than you." My inability to get the jewelry out of the safe in the dream or to pull the safe off the closet shelf represents my shedding of the need for external markers to legitimize my existence. In the dream, the jewelry burned, and, once on the hill with my family, I felt at peace—I had no need for it anymore.

Also, I think the burning of my house in the dream was a message to me about the over-emphasis I have placed on material wealth and accumulation.

The American dream seemingly offers people a short cut to individuation through bypassing the plunge into the darkness and offering a sense of false security.

I began collecting art as part of an , unconscious desire to fit in with people I deemed sophisticated. I thought that if I surrounded myself with enough beauty, particularly beauty deemed culturally appropriate, I could erase my past. Living in my house surrounded by art has provided security. It has represented that I will never be judged unsophisticated, lacking in taste, unintelligent, and uneducated—in a word, low class. A description of myself I would be most afraid to hear is, "She has no class." My mom and I always thought one of the biggest insults to anyone was to accuse them of having no class. In fact, when we would see someone dressed unfashionably or acting in a way we deemed unsophisticated, we used to say, N. C.; this meant no class. In every dwelling I have lived in as an adult, I have attempted to convey a sense of refinement that deep inside I feel I lack. I have made a greater effort to make this statement with the house I live in now. The burning of this house is another stripping away of the layers of wounding that has restricted my life.

However, the fact that "Crossing Over" was saved from the fire means that only part of me has purchased art and other material objects to impress others. Another part of me has a strong pull toward beauty and the painting represents that passion. Just as a wounded part of me needed recognition through class ascension, my soul had nudged me in the direction of higher education because I have a true passion to learn. Earning a doctoral degree, I thought, would bring me status, but in the process I learned about the real reasons I set out on this initiatory journey. I crossed over into new territory in my soul with more self-acceptance and a deeper understanding of my gifts as well as my shortcomings.

Mythic Components of the American Dream

Although the particulars of my story are unique, the climb up the class ladder is a familiar, if not a common, American story. However, the dark side of the story is not often brought to light. The story of upward mobility has such broad appeal because of its mythic quality. The American Dream myth supports the belief that America is a land of opportunity in which all are able to succeed through hard work and determination. Success, according to the dream, is measured by professional achievement along with material wealth and accumulation. The dream promises that those people born in the working class, and even those born into poverty, can achieve higher class status if they are willing to sacrifice, through force of will and effort, for the goal of upward mobility. Also embedded in the dream is the belief that those who are not able to rise in the class system are lacking in ambition and possess some character flaw that inhibits their ability to achieve higher status.

For those from lower- or working-class origins, this dream can serve as a guiding myth and provide inspiration for them to live differently from their parents. In the process of striving for a better life, this dream encourages people to believe they will be able to reach their highest potential. As is suggested in the literature, the dream is deeply embedded in the American consciousness and adherence to it crosses racial, class, socioeconomic, and political lines. The power in this dream is that it aligns with the human tendency toward growth and individuation. Erikson (1950) and Loevinger (1976) theorize that human beings continue to grow throughout their lives by navigating through several distinct stages of identity development. Horney (1950, p. 15) states that, "Man by his very nature and of his own accord, strives toward self-realization, and that his set of values evolves from such striving." This dream provides a framework for growth and also can provide meaning for the struggle of hard work and sacrifice.

The quest to achieve the American dream also is related to the hero's quest tale. Joseph Campbell (1949, pp. 30-35) asserts that all heroes' quest tales are initiatory journeys that involve several key elements: the longing, the call, the departure, tests and ordeals, guides or mentors to assist the hero through the difficult tasks, the arrival, the return, and the boon. The journey up the class ladder for the lower- or working-class person can be interpreted as a hero's quest tale. People from humble origins are the heroes or seekers. They feel a longing for a better life and heed the call of the American dream that promises more status, privileges, and comforts.

The call is heeded and they depart from their family of origin and set out on the journey to have a better life

Many of the destructive underlying tenets of the American Dream remain unconscious in the American psyche.

than that of their parents. They face the difficult task of higher education and are often overwhelmed by its demands. They are given guidance from a few mentors along the way, yet face several obstacles before they are able to complete the tasks required for this stage of the journey. They meet the challenges of completing their educations and breaking into professions that they had never dreamed existed. They arrive in the professional middle class and return to the world with new knowledge. Their new knowledge and skills are rewarded by substantial financial gain (the boon), and they carry their new identity into the world.

The American Dream has many components of hero's initiatory journey, yet it seems to fail on several important levels. Those who ascend from the working class are left with feelings of deep inferiority and shame that they attempt to cover with a myriad of maladaptive defensive structures. So what are the shadow aspects of this dream, and what happens when people become mired in shame that they are unable to acknowledge or express? What stunts their ability to individuate? In choosing to climb the class ladder they have taken considerable risk and made sacrifices, yet they

may be left feeling empty. The hidden, detrimental aspects of this dream that cause those faithful to it to go awry are many.

The journey of achievement of this dream and the resulting upward mobility often lie in direct conflict with the soul's journey and may serve to reinforce adaptive identities that are created along the path. James Hollis (2005, p. 11) says, "The soul is what moves and directs the total organism toward survival, growth, development, and meaning." He also interprets Jung's vision of individuation or the soul's journey as follows:

Individuation is the lifelong project of becoming more nearly the whole person we were meant to be—what the gods intended, not the parents, or the tribe, or, especially the easily intimidated or inflated ego. (p. 10)

The reasons that people set out on the path of achieving the American dream often do not align with this definition of individuation. Although people may go through the journey of upward mobility and develop personally along the way, the goals of this dream that hinder their development are those that emphasize the acquisition of material wealth and elevated status. It is not implied in the goals of the American dream that the wealth or recognition gained are for the betterment of the culture as a whole. The new knowledge that is often sought after is not for personal enrichment, but for elevated status. These goals are not aligned with the inner life; instead, they satisfy outward appearances of success. The dream is often sought after for the purpose of showing others that it has been achieved. Those who pursue wealth, material accumulation, and the status the dream promises may be left feeling conflicted and unfulfilled.

Jung (1963) explains that human beings have a tendency toward meaning-making. He says, "Meaninglessness inhibits the fullness of life, and is therefore equivalent to illness. Meaning makes a great many things endurable—perhaps everything" (p. 340). Upward mobility did not bring the anticipated level of meaning to the lives of m participants, and undoubtedly others as well

The soul's journey requires that one step out of adaptive identity into the darkness or unknown and open the self to the mystery of what life holds. Adaptive identities or false selves often emerge as the result of overwhelming experiences. The culture and family of origin that people are born into often determines the lenses through which they will view the world. These lenses are distorted. People develop false selves to protect themselves from being hurt or merely just to survive, and the false self restricts experiences. On the other hand, one's soul or true self embodies a much larger purpose for the individual beyond the limitations of family history or the cultural expectations. The option of ignoring the needs of the soul and adopting cultural values that seemingly guarantee happiness and fulfillment can certainly be alluring, but fulfilling the soul's desire often requires stepping away from conformity.

The American dream seemingly offers people a short cut to individuation through bypassing the plunge into the darkness and offering a sense of false security. The collective culture has placed value on particular experiences and professions. For instance, medical or legal careers often are rewarded with high status as well as financial rewards. A person may ignore the nudging of the soul towards another occupational path and opt for the goals deemed lofty by the culture. Becoming a doctor or lawyer fulfills the American dream, but the pursuit of an acting career might be deemed silly by the collective culture, particularly if it did not involve earning a large salary. Those who fear heeding the whisper of the soul's voice can fall prey to cultural expectations. One must withdraw from the compliance to cultural norms to truly individuate.

However, as indicated above, pursuit of the American dream for those from the working class is not detrimental in and of itself. Some people can lose their way on the journey and develop a dysfunctional relationship to wealth and

appearances, but others may find that, in spite of the dark side of the dream, their adherence to it leads toward individuation. For instance, while one may seek higher education as a means to gain status and position, the educational process may lead to a greater understanding of the true self. Also, the professions that people choose that align with cultural

Although success is culturally measured by material consumption, professional success, and achievement, adherence to these values may undermine a client's ability to ameliorate the toxic affect of hidden shame.

values of success may prove to be individuating. However, the danger is that the status and wealth that are often a result of these choices may place people in a life of inauthentic fulfillment. They may use the comforts and luxuries that often accompany achievement of the American dream as crutch to ignore their soul's yearning for something different.

Class Identity Shame and Psychotherapy

Since the American dream is deeply embedded in the American psyche and is so inextricably linked to class identity shame, those who work in the profession of psychology are in a unique position to help others acknowledge, understand, and work toward shifting their class identity shame. Those who turn toward psychotherapy for help with mental health issues are impacted by taboos that surround both class identity and shame. Not only are clients affected by the code of silence, clinicians may be unaware of their own unwillingness to transgress cultural taboos because of their own unexamined shame. It is particularly important that clinicians

understand that their clients may be hiding intense feelings of shame and inferiority regarding class identity. Although family dynamics are important clinical considerations, the impact of the culture's unwritten rules about class and shame must be addressed and acknowledged as well.

Class shame wounding can be deftly covered up, offering no clue to its impact on the client. Upwardly mobile clients, who have obtained the material trappings of success and have achieved professional competence, may have defensive armoring that makes detecting shame difficult. These clients have often been positively reinforced for having climbed the social ladder and may present with a false air of confidence. Denial and avoidance of class shame is well practiced, and the clients themselves may be unaware they are carrying it.

Wurmser (1987) theorizes that shame undermines the relationship between client and therapist. He did not examine shame as it relates to class identity, but discusses the general impact of shame on the therapeutic relationship. He posits that the therapist's inherent position of power over the client exacerbates feelings of existing shame. Those who have been upwardly mobile in this culture are particularly vulnerable to these power dynamics. Wurmser argues that the clients' defenses against shame can trigger shame in the clinicians. Both the clinician and client could enter into an inextricable shame spiral that destroys the relationship.

People who experience class identity shame often avoid feeling their shame by using a myriad of defensive behaviors that can evoke shameful feelings in the clinician. Although clinicians may not carry shame specifically related to class, their unique shame scripts can still be activated by clients who suffer from class wounding. Clinicians experiencing shame are less able to hold an empathetic container for the client. Wurmser (1987) theorizes that clinicians disrupt or contaminate the healing process if they are unaware of their shame scripts and defensive strategies.

In order to help ameliorate the impact of class identity shame on clients, clinicians must explore their own shame wounding and defensive strategies. Wurmser (89-90) suggested that clinicians feel shame about being ashamed; therefore this affect often remains underground. Clinicians need to establish safe containers with other therapists, within which they can freely express shame and the dark feelings that surround it. Clinicians who do their own shame work are better equipped to understand the shame of others.

Clients may often be negatively impacted by their adherence to the American dream. Clinicians need to be aware of their relationship to the American values of success and their feelings about class stratification. Although success is culturally measured by material consumption, professional success, and achievement, adherence to these values may undermine a client's ability to ameliorate the toxic affect of hidden shame. If clinicians are attached to the American formula for success, they may unconsciously reinforce their clients' accomplishments and bypass the clients' true need to confront class shame wounding.

Clinicians from all class backgrounds would benefit from an examination of their own biases and an understanding of collective stereotyping targeted at class groups. Clients who are hiding class shame may not benefit from validation of their achievements; they need assistance understanding their motivations to climb up the class ladder. Additionally, clients who have been upwardly mobile may internalize cultural negative biases and use them as motivation to ascend to a higher level in the class structure. Negative identification with their class backgrounds creates internal conflict that feeds their defensive system. If clinicians are from professional middle-class or upper-class backgrounds, they may not be aware of the impact of cultural biases on the working class or the shadow aspects of class ascension.

Transgressing Cultural Taboos Surrounding Class Identity

Educators must be trained to under-stand the dynamics of the class shame experience to recognize it in their students and in themselves. They are in a unique position to transmit and perpetuate the values of the culture, but they also have the power to shape these values. Educators need to be sensitive to the plight of the working class when selecting texts and creating units of study.

Students of all levels, kindergarten through college, and from all social classes, poverty through wealth, would benefit from challenging their basic assumptions about opportunity, wealth, status, upward mobility, achievement, and success. Students will not be provided this opportunity if educators are not trained to understand the taboo that exists about acknowledging the shadow of the class structure. Also, educators need to be aware of their own assumptions and biases that assist in perpetuating the social order. Since class (unlike race and gender) is not immediately visible, students may be unaware that they have any class shame.

In addition, educational counselors, school administrators, and teachers unconsciously pledge allegiance to the American dream when working-class occupations are openly discouraged and college preparatory classes are touted as the only means to success (Nieto, 2002). Education is used as a vehicle for class ascension in this culture. The American dream myth that success is based on upward mobility, wealth, and achievement brings into question the worth of individuals and groups who do not hold esteemed positions in the culture. As revealed in Sennett and Cobb's (1972) and Rubin's studies (1976), members of the working class believe they have inherited their class position based on the inferiority of family members from past generations.

Educators who are unaware of their biases or underlying inferiority scripts are inclined to react to their students' defensive behaviors against class shame. John Bradshaw (1988, p. 12) points out that "shame begets shame." Just as Wurmser theorizes that the relationship between therapist and client is contaminated by unacknowledged shame, teach-ers and student relationships are vulnerable to these dynamics as well. Since teachers have such a broad base of influence, they need training to understand their own inferiority scripts in order to provide safe emotional containers for student learning.

The American Dream is a source of national pride and certainly can assist in providing hope and also, a psychological structure and framework for those who choose and are able to climb up the class ladder. However, many of the destructive underlying tenets of the American Dream remain unconscious in the American psyche. The American dream implies that all people have an equal opportunity for self-improvement, which places the responsibility for upward mobility on the individual. Acknowledging that class oppression is a social issue, rather than a problem created by the individual, is a step toward healing the wounds of class shame that are hidden. All those affected by class stratification will benefit by acknowledging and examining the shadow of the American Dream and its connection to the internal experiences of shame that surround class identity.

Notes

[1] The idea that shame must be acknowledged and experienced in order for it to turn toward a more positive affect was presented by Aftab Omer in course lecture at the Institute of Imaginal Studies at the Angela Center in Santa Rosa, CA, on September 14, 2001.

[2] Aftab Omer, course notes, July 2001. I am indebted to Aftab Omer, president and founder of Meridian University, formerly known as the Institute of Imaginal Studies, for providing insight into the importance of developing capacities in order to transmute negative affects.

[3] Aftab Omer, personal communication. April 2, 2006. Aftab Omer assisted me in understanding that the experiencing of shame is integral to the transmutation of affects into capacities resulting in authentic power.

[4] Aftab Omer, course notes, July 9, 2001.

References

Bradshaw, J. (1988). *Healing the shame that binds you.* Deerfield Beach, FL: HCI Publishing.

Butsch, R. (2003). "Ralph, fred, archie, and homer: Why American television keeps re-creating the white male working-class buffoon." In G. Dines & J. Humez (Eds.), *Gender, race, and class in the media: A text reader* (pp. 575-585). Thousand Oaks, CA: Sage Publications.

Campbell, J. (1949). *The hero with a thousand faces*. NY: Princeton University Press.

Cullen, J. (2003). *The American dream: A short history of an idea that shaped a nation*. New York: Oxford University Press.

Demott, B. (1990). *The imperial middle: Why Americans can't think straight about class*. New Haven, CT: Yale University Press.

Ehrenreich, B. (1989). *Fear of falling: The inner life of the middle class*. New York: Harper Perennial.

Erikson, E. (1950). *Childhood and society*. New York: W. W. Norton & Company.

Erikson, E. (1959) *Identity and the Life Cycle*. New York: W. W. Norton.

Freire, P. (1970). *Pedagogy of the oppressed*. New York: Continuum.

Fussell, P. (1983). *Class: A guide through the American status system*. New York: Simon & Schuster.

Grimes, M., J. Morris. (1997). *Caught in the middle: Contradictions in the lives of sociologists from working-class backgrounds*. Westport, CT: Praeger.

Hochschild, J. (1995). *Facing up to the American dream: Race, class, and the soul of the nation*. Princeton, NJ: Princeton University Press.

Hollis, J. (2005). *Finding meaning in the second half of life*. New York: Gotham Books.

hooks, b. (2000). *Where we stand: class matters*. New York: Routledge.

Horney, K. (1950). *Neurosis and human growth: The struggle toward self realization*. New York: W.W. Norton.

Jung, C. (1963). *Memories, dreams, and reflections*. New York: Vintage Books.

Kaufman, G. (1989). *The psychology of shame: Theory and treatment of shame-based syndromes*. New York: Springer.

Kaufman, G. (1992). *Shame: The power of caring*. Rochester, VT: Schenkman.

Kaufman, G., & L. Raphael, L.. (1996). *Coming out of shame: Transforming gay and lesbian lives*. New York: Doubleday.

Lareau, A. (2003). *Unequal childhoods: Class, race, and family life*. Berkeley, CA: University of California Press.

Law, C. (1985). Introduction. In C. L. Dews & C. Law (Eds.), *This fine place so far from home* (pp. 4-24). Philadelphia, PA: Temple University Press.

Lewis, H. (1971). *Shame and guilt in neurosis*. New York: International University Presses.

Lewis, H. (1987a). The role of shame in depression over the life span. In H. Lewis (Ed.) *The role of shame in symptom formation* (pp. 29-50). Hillsdale, NJ: Lawrence Erlbaum.

Lewis, H. (1987b). Shame and the narcissistic personality. In D. Nathanson (Ed.), *The many faces of shame* (pp. 93-132). New York: The Guilford Press.

Lewis, H. (1987c). Shame, the sleeper in psychopathology. In H. Lewis (Ed.), *The role of shame in symptom formation* (pp. 29-50). Hillsdale, NJ: Lawrence Erlbaum.

Linkon, S. (1999). *Teaching working class*. Amherst, MA: University of Massachusetts Press.

Loevinger, J. (1976). *Ego development*. San Francisco, CA: Jossey-Bass Publisher.

Morrison, A. (1996). *The culture of shame*. New York: Ballantine Books.

Nathanson, D. (1992). *Shame and pride: affect, sex, and the birth of the self*. New York: W. W. Norton.

Nieto, S. (2002). *Affirming diversity: The sociopolitical context of multicultural education*. New York: Longman.

Obama, B. (2008, January 29). Reclaiming the american dream. Speech retrieved from http://www.barackobama.net

Ohmann, R. (2003). Teaching historically. In R. Ohmann (Ed.), *Commercialization of the university, the professions, and print culture* (pp. 49-77). Middletown CT: Wesleyan University Press.

Policar, H. (2006). *Class identity: The experience of shame in realizing the American dream* (Unpublished doctoral dissertation). Institute of Imaginal Studies, Petaluma, CA.

Retzinger, S. (1987). Resentment and laughter: Video studies of the shame-rage spiral. In H. Lewis (Ed.), *The role of shame in symptom formation* (pp. 151-182). Hillsdale, NJ: Lawrence Erlbaum.

Rifkin, J. (2004). *The European dream: How Europe's vision of the future is quietly eclipsing the American dream*. New York: Jeremy Tarcher.

Rubin, L. (1976). *Worlds of pain: Life in the working-class family*. New York: Basic Books.

Scharrer, E. (2001). From wise to foolish: The portrayal of the sit-com father, 1950-1990's. *Journal of broadcasting and electronic media, 45,* 23-55.

Scheff, T. (2003). Shame and self in society. *Symbolic interaction, 26,* 239-262.

Scheff, T. (1987). The shame-rage spiral: A Case Study of an Interminable Quarrel." In H. Lewis (Ed.) *The role of shame in symptom formation* (pp. 109-149). Hillsdale, NJ: Lawrence Erlbaum.

Sennett, R., & J. Cobb. (1972). *The hidden injuries of class*. New York: W. W. Norton.

Tokarczyk, M., & Fay, E.. (1993). Introduction. In M. Tokarcyzk & E. Fay (Eds.), *Working-class women in the academy: Laborers in the knowledge factory* (pp. 3-24). Amherst, MA: University of Massachusetts Press.

Wurmser, L. (1987). The veiled companion of narcissism. In D. Nathanson (Ed.), *The many faces of shame* (pp. 64-92). New York: The Guilford Press.

Zandy, J. (1995). Introduction. In J. Zandy (Ed.), *Liberating memory: Our work and working-class consciousness* (pp. 1-14). New Brunswick, NJ: Rutgers University Press.

Time
That ancient bard
Never repeating a story
Always coming up
With new editions
Of familiar songs

Michael Sheffield

Photo: Katrina Martin Davenport, www.octoberphotography.etsy.com

Therapy Dreams

Barbara Loeb

Combining fantasy and archetypal images, "Therapy Dreams" are a subjective representation of the author's experiences with her psychotherapist, "Jason" (not his real name), with whom she had weekly sessions for about two years. Although I, the author, am fully awake in the process of writing these pieces, I am reporting on the images that appear in my mind, as they flow through pen onto paper.

In "Therapy Dreams," two common phenomena of psychotherapy are represented in an imaginary way:

Transference: First identified by Freud, the client projects onto the therapist feelings about important figures from the past, such as the clients' parents. These feelings often formed at a pre-verbal age. Also with transference, clients' behavior in the therapist's office typically mirrors behavior in the world. The therapist uses transference reactions to guide the client to realizations about behavior patterns.

Barbara Loeb is studying for an M.A. in Integral Counseling Psychology at the California Institute of Integral Studies. Psychology is Barbara's second career. Before entering CIIS, she earned an MBA from Stanford University and worked for over 20 years in marketing management at major Bay Area corporations. In addition to taking classes, she is currently writing a young adult novel, entitled *Lissy and the New York Dream*.

Projection: The client projects onto the therapist disturbing feelings from within. With projection, the client does not have to cope with the feelings, unconsciously hoping the therapist will catch and contain them.

In "Therapy Dreams," Jason appears as a powerful, majestic, distant, lofty figure, including a king and an angel. While Jason is often angry and demanding, the client yearns for his recognition, even love. Applying the principle of transference, this image of Jason reveals how the client/author must have viewed her parents when she was young. At the same time, one might wonder whether these reactions reveal projection, the author's unsurfaced feelings inside herself, such as anger or need to achieve high standards.

By representing the psychotherapy experience subjectively, the author hopes to communicate the feelings that therapy generates. And perhaps it becomes apparent that Jason is not only the author's guide. He is also her muse.

Therapy Dream: Union Square

I'm one of the crowd, craning my neck to see you, jostled by the people around me, pushing, elbowing, shout-

> **"Therapy Dreams" reveals child-like emotional dependency and profound longing for connection with an important, larger-than life being, who is also symbolic of the adult's longing for connection with the true self.**

ing "Jason." I want you to pick me out of all the people there. I'm wearing my red satin cape and red leotard and white tights and black patent leather tap shoes and a silver top hat. I dance because I hope you'll notice me. Other people are dancing too—Indian whirling dervishes, contortionists, ballerinas. A clown is twisting balloons into anima-shapes, a bearded man in a kilt is playing the bagpipes and a silver-haired woman in a tie-dye tunic is beating on a tambourine. We're all in Union Square and we all want you.

Then magically you pick me, flick your finger at me, that's how I know. I drop to the ground and then I rise. I'm glad I wore my cape and my tap shoes, maybe that's why you noticed me. Then you throw me a golden rope so I can join you on your cloud. I climb the rope and can't stop grinning. My heart is beating fast. You pat me on the back as I reach your throne. You sit and I kneel at your feet. You talk of many things—feelings and repressions and peace within my soul and you also talk of your life on the island where you live with your wife. I soak it all in, rapt, like a plant thirsty for water; sprinkle my leaves and maybe someday it will reach my roots. I don't want this to end, but I know it will. You tap your watch. I don't want to get up, I refuse, it can't be time already. You pull me up and twist my cape so I almost choke. Your face turns dark and you thunder, "Out. Now." I start to sob. I just want a few more minutes.

Obediently, I turn away. But even so, you pull out a whip from an oak drawer beneath your throne. You pull out a whip and slash it across my back, once, twice, three times. I scream in pain. I didn't expect this. It hasn't happened before.

Humbly I go. I gingerly place my hands on the golden rope and slide back down to Union Square. Along the way, I pass your next patient on her way up. She has long blonde hair and is wearing a white leotard trimmed with gold sequins, her breasts stick out like cones. I melt into the crowd at Union Square

and find my sleeping bag. I lay it out in a corner, on the grass near the stairs. I'll sleep here tonight because I know you're not far away. I feel the welts in my back. They sting but the good part

And yet I know what I'm really searching for--as I paddle up and down the shore--what I keep looking for, as I stop at all the islands, I keep hoping I'll land on one island, and when I do, fireworks will explode and a marching band will play, because then finally I'll know, finally I'll find: myself.

is, I feel the hurt and it reminds me of you.

Therapy Dream: Swimming

The sea is gray and choppy, cold and salty. I'm wearing only my royal blue nylon tank suit, the same one I wore when I was the Suburban Swim League backstroke champion, girls 12 and under. I'm floating and bobbing and get salty water in my mouth that I have to spit out. I dive under the water and see translucent fish shimmer by, ruby and bronze and emerald. Then I soar back up to the surface, take a deep gulp of air and realize I'm back where I started.

I swim all day, breast stroking, passing an island with hula girls and ukulele music and another island with growling tigers in cages and another one with a red brick schoolhouse, smoke spewing from the chimney. I paddle and don't know where to stop. I salute each island that I pass. Then I come to another island with a cement high-rise building and an American flag outside and televisions blaring to watch President Obama address the country about the

wars in Pakistan and North Korea. I'd like to watch this too.

I swim to shore. My skin is salty and I find a blanket in a corner of the beach, a frayed dirty brown blanket from Yin Sang's yoga class. It's enough to keep me warm. Hanging on an apple tree is a powder pink velour tracksuit and Puma tennis shoes and a magenta spandex top with sequins. Later I find out that Jason left these clothes for me. He knows my size, XSmall. I shiver into the tracksuit and creep into the building. A guard is snoozing at the desk and doesn't see me. I stop at the elevator and don't know which floor to go to. Or maybe it doesn't matter.

I try the third floor, because "3rd time's a charm" rings in my head. I tiptoe past a room where women are making Easter hats, sewing floppy cloth flowers and rhinestones and velvet ribbons on them. They have spent many years together in this room. They chat as they sew, some of them with thread in their mouths. I pass another room with high school students bent over their desks, writing in blue books with fountain pens, girls in plaid skirts, boys in black corduroy trousers and black leather tie shoes, polished so they shine like a new Maserati.

This isn't what I'm looking for. I take the stairs up to the tenth floor, all the way to the top. I like how my legs ache after the climb.

The top floor is a loft, just one large room and at the center is Jason in bed with his wife. It's a canopy bed with deep purple velvet curtains at the side, so they can pull the curtains closed when they make love. He has his arm around her and they're laughing. They don't see me. I slink in, hide under the bed. I strain to hear what they talk about—the Ingmar Bergman movie they watched tonight, their Sunday picnic on Mt. Tam, the trip to Japan they want to take next summer. I cough and he gets up, discovers me under the bed and reaches out to me. I grab his arms as he pulls me up. I start to cry and he comforts me, leads me to a midnight blue velvet chair in the corner, puts a screen in front of the chair so that his wife doesn't see us. He strokes my hand as I cry. I don't try to stop the tears for the love I never had and my frantic search to find a new home. He gets the keys to his car, a cherry red Camry, and says he'll take me somewhere he thinks I'll like.

I sit beside him in the car and bask in the silence. Warmth flows through my body like honey and flushes my cheeks. He drives fast, swerving in and out of traffic, passing cars, on his way to our destination. Finally he pulls into the driveway of a small cottage, with a lily-bordered walkway leading to the oak door. He turns an iron key in the lock, opens the door and leads me in.

I twirl around the room. It's what I wanted but didn't know I wanted until today. A living room with knit rugs and a pine bookcase filled with antique silver pitchers and tattered paperback classics like Jane Eyre and A Tale of Two Cities. A pink wooden desk in the corner, trimmed in gold, overlooking the garden, where Spanish moss drips from the trees. Rosebud print curtains and matching pillows. I waltz around the room, cradling each piece of furniture, afraid to think this is really mine.

He must go back to his wife now, for she is waiting for him at their banquet table with platters of capon, baskets of grapes, jugs of wine. I'm not sure how long I'll stay in this cottage or if it's really what I'm looking for. Soon I might have to lock the door, drop the key off at Jason's and plunge back into the choppy gray ocean, still bobbing up and down, paddling, changing from breaststroke to freestyle to sidestroke until I find a resting place. As I swim, I think of him, and see him in a sea green tunic and sandals, on a beach with a basket of fruit. I keep searching for him. And yet I know what I'm really searching for--as I paddle up and down the shore--what I keep looking for, as I stop at all the islands, I keep hoping I'll land on one island, and when I do, fireworks will explode and a marching band will play, because then finally I'll know, finally I'll find: myself.

Therapy Dream: Gold

This time, he'll come in on a cloud, wearing a robe like an angel, bring-ing a basket lined with silver silk and filled with chocolates and pieces of gold. He'll bring the basket to me as I sit waiting, on a red plaid blanket by the river, looking up at the clouds in the

Photo: Astrid Berg, www.astridberg.com

sky and wondering when he'll come. I wait here everyday. Every morning, I rise from my narrow bed, take a sip of water from the glass on my pine nightstand, go to my small kitchen and pack my basket. My kitchen counter is made of tiles with a cherry pattern, and I have a red checked tablecloth on the table and chrome chairs with round red vinyl seats, like the ones in diners I used to frequent in high school. I glance out my kitchen window at the marigolds in my small garden. Once in awhile, I water the flowers or sprinkle them with plant food. Mostly they grow without my help.

I pack my wooden picnic basket with apples from the farm next door and a piece of white cheddar cheese and sesame crackers from the small grocery store a block from my house, the one with a wooden floor and wire shelves. I don't usually go to big grocery stores in the town, 10 miles away, because I don't need much food anymore and avoid cooking when I can. I take a red checked broadcloth napkin from the drawer under my kitchen counter. It's filled with cloth napkins in many patterns. Some of my favorites are: the yellow Provencal pattern with miniature roses, the burgundy polished cotton napkins with a thin burgundy ribbon on the border, and the red checked fringed napkins I chose today. I like to use cloth napkins instead of paper.

Everyday I walk to the river because I don't know when he'll come. If it's raining, I walk anyway and wear an Army-green slicker and carry a big umbrella—the umbrella I got from my mother's house after she died—its brave nylon reproducing Monet's water lilies. On rainy days, I also put a small collapsible umbrella in my picnic basket in case the winds bend the spokes of my big umbrella. I don't want to get wet.

I pass my neighbors' cottages and bungalows. Today Philip's yard is shorn trim from faithful Sunday mowings. His small terrier dog plays behind his white picket fence. The dog yaps at me but stops when I say, "Quiet, Molly." Then I trod by the mailman, and he winks at me. I've had the same mailman for all five years I've been here and once he asked me to meet him at Bella Casa, the only restaurant in town for a plate of spaghetti and a glass of red wine. I said no. I had letters to write

My head is still bowed but my heart is throbbing and my eyes are wet with tears because I have had this treasure box since my youth, and now it's broken

that night and, after that, I wanted to sit by the fire and do a few yoga poses and read my new glossy fashion magazine, the only one I get, one a month.

I come to the river, and today the bank is dry. We haven't had rain in awhile. I put down my blanket and align it so that the long end is parallel to the river, then find stones to put in each corner so that blanket stays flat even if the wind gusts. I put my basket down next to the blanket and wait. I didn't bring a watch, and I left my cell phone at home. I can tell what time it is by how high the sun is in the sky.

I look out at the river. A raft of tourists floats by. Their guide, a shirtless man with long black hair and curly beard, does most of the rowing. His taut shoulder muscles glisten with sweat. The tourists in their tee shirts and Bermuda shorts and sun hats snap pictures. I wave at them, and one of them, a skinny boy with a blonde crew cut, waves back.

The sun is overhead. It must be noon. Jason hasn't come. I keep waiting. It's been a few days or maybe more. I stopped counting. I know he'll come again. That's why I wait.

And then a cloud swoops by and lands on the riverbank. The cloud dissolves, and Jason is inside. He walks over to me and touches my head, then strokes my long thin hair. I start to cry. And he says, "Shhh."

He is wearing the white angel robe and sandals, just like last time. Today he asks me to reach into his basket and take what I want, a chocolate or a piece of gold. I want to take them all, every piece in the basket, but I can only take one, so I don't even ask. I pick a piece of gold and hold it in my fingers. This one is smooth and oval. I have others that are gold nuggets, and some are little gold bars and, once in awhile, I choose a chocolate square. When I get home, I will put a label on my piece, and write the date with a green ink pen, so I remember when I got it. Then I will put it in a drawer in my pine dresser. It's a big drawer, big enough to hold a dozen sweaters or my collection of frayed flannel nightgowns or all my jeans and yoga pants. But I save this drawer for my pieces of gold and chocolate, the ones I get from Jason.

I grip the gold stone in my hand and clench my fingers around it. I hold it in front of my throbbing heart. Jason watches me and presses his hand on top of mine, and I wonder if he can feel my heart, too. His soft brown eyes gaze at

me. I stopped crying awhile ago. Then I look down at the piece of gold and run my fingers over it. This will be all I have left of him. Until he comes again.

Therapy Dream: Treasure Box

I go to his office wearing a pinafore and carrying a treasure box. It's a small box, decorated with lace and tiny satin roses and gold butterflies. I carry it with both hands. I don't want to drop it. He has the key.

I press the button next to the placard with Jason's name, and wait in the hall. It's a long hall, with bentwood chairs lined up against each wall, and an Oriental runner down the middle. There's a Nubian servant at one end, strong, glistening bald head, ebony skin. When it's your turn, you take his arm and he leads to you to the room, Jason's room.

Now Jason opens the door. He's wearing a long velvet robe and carrying a scepter engraved with the names of master therapists, like Winnicott and Maslow and Klein. I kneel before Jason. My head is bowed but my arms hold up the treasure box as an offering. I hope he has the key.

He takes the box and twists it in his hands, turning it over and over. He reaches into his pocket and tries a key, but it is way too big for the lock. He turns and looks in his desk drawer and comes up with a handful of keys and tries each one. None of them fit.

His face grows dark, and he grabs the treasure box from me and throws it to the marble floor. He stomps on it until it shatters. My head is still bowed but my heart is throbbing and my eyes are wet with tears because I have had this treasure box since my youth, and now it's broken. He jumps on the treasure box, then takes out a hammer and pounds it into a thousand pieces. I wail. I see inside there was a tiny crystal horse, like the one on my Great Aunt Lizzy's farm, a tiny figurine that has escaped his hammer. I crawl to where the treasure box is and pocket the tiny horse, hoping Jason won't see me.

But now he grows angry, grabs the horse from between my clutched fingers, and pounds it too. I'm empty, broken. The session is over. It's time to go. Jason writes in his appointment book with a long quill pen. I'll see him

the same time next week. The Nubian slave enters, takes my arms and leads me from the room. Jason yells at him to come back when he's done leading me away. "Don't forget to clean up this mess," he thunders at the slave.

Out on the sidewalk, my rubber sandals scuff against the pavement, and a pebble rubs between my toes. But then, across the street, I see David--my teacher, my advisor; I want him for my friend. David waves to me, and I run, against the light. A taxicab almost runs me down. David puts his arm around my shoulders, pulls out a handkerchief and dries my tears. He doesn't know where I've been. He leads me to Union Square, and we sit on a stone bench. Shoppers and businessmen hurry by, but he looks into my eyes. I tell him about my treasure box and the tiny horse that are gone. And then from his pocket, he pulls out a tiny crystal horse, just like the one Jason shattered, only this one is on a silver chain. He fastens the clasp of the chain around my neck, and I hide the chain inside my shirt. No one can see it now.

I'll go to Jason next week and he won't see the tiny horse. We can talk about the treasure box and the other things he's broken for me: my Raggedy Ann he shredded, my doll closet he sawed in two, my miniature tea set he confiscated and shipped to his daughter in Japan. But now I have a secret, a new tiny horse, like the one he stole from me but better: it has a silver chain and it came from David. I hope Jason won't find it and take it away. I'll keep talking as I always do, but a little voice inside my head will be watching and whispering, "Don't tell him about the horse, or he'll hurt you to get it. You have a way out you never had before. So keep on talking and feel the tiny horse nestled near your heart that beats so hard when you talk to him. Keep talking and bowing, but now you know you have a life, a life outside him, and trust the tiny horse because finally it's time. The tiny horse will show you now, after all these years, finally to a new way."

The Erotics of Accountability: A Psychological Approach

Anne Coelho

One bright day on March 3, 1986, seven young men set out on a journey with hopes of joining the fight against apartheid in South Africa. Not experienced in how to join the underground forces for freedom, they placed their trust in a man who spoke with authority and experience. He encouraged them, and even promised guns and transportation for a plan to raid the local police station in their township of Guguletu. Unfortunately, this man was an askari, an anti-apartheid activist who had himself been captured and forced into service for the police. The arrangement that he made with the Guguletu Seven, as they came to be known, was a set-up. Shortly after the seven set out on their journey, they were ambushed by 25 police, some of them also black South Africans. The young men were massacred by the police that day, even as they surrendered and did

Anne Coelho, Ph.D., received her doctorate from Meridian University, formerly known as the Institute of Imaginal Studies and a Masters in Religious Education from University of San Diego. Anne's background includes considerable work related to social justice and alliance building issues. As a consultant and trainer, she teaches workshops and trainings on restorative justice and accountability as well as diversity issues. Anne taught at the Institute of Imaginal Studies from 2005 through 2008. She is an associate of TODOS Alliance Building Institute, an organization dedicated to building personal and organizational skills and capacities in order to create a more just and equitable society.

not put up a fight. Gruesome video footage filmed by the police aired on the television news that day, and it was in that way that some of the young men's families learned of their deaths.

The askari involved in the killing of the Guguletu Seven was one of many black South Africans who were recruited or pressured into service of the apartheid era law enforcement agencies, some as undercover operatives and others as police officers. There was great animosity toward these South Africans for the betrayals and violence that they participated in towards their own brothers and sisters. Thapelo Mbelo was one such man who betrayed his people. He was one of the 25 police who ambushed the Guguletu Seven. The story of his efforts to come to terms with his involvement in the massacre of the Guguletu Seven was highlighted in Frances Reid and Deborah Hoffman's (1997) video documentary, "Long Night's Journey into Day." Ten years after the Guguletu Seven were killed, the new South African government under the leadership of Nelson Mandela provided the opportunity for reckoning and beginning to heal some of the wounds of the apartheid years. Mandela's government created the Truth and Reconciliation Commission in order to facilitate an intensive process of uncovering and unraveling the events of those painful

and tragic years. The Truth and Reconciliation Commission (TRC) provided the opportunity for those who committed war crimes to apply for amnesty in exchange for the truth of their actions and recognition of the harm that they caused. Thapelo Mbelo was one of two police officers involved in the massacre of the Guguletu Seven who applied to the for amnesty. He explained that he did so because "I have to face my black brothers and sisters. That's a daily thing. (The white officer) is going to the bar with his white friends. We are not on par with each other."[1]

During the apartheid years, Mbelo admitted that he had to numb himself with alcohol in order to act out the violence that was an everyday part of his employment. But in contrast to the numbness that allowed him to avoid being affected by what was happening Mbelo deeply participated in the Truth and Reconciliation Commission public hearing about the violence toward the Guguletu Seven. Even more remarkably, he courageously went beyond the requirements of the TRC and met with the mothers of the Guguletu Seven. He sat before the mothers and admitted to them what he had done, acknowledging the evil in his heart, then listened with his face twitching and down-turned in shame as they expressed rage and grief cursed him, and vented about what he had done to their lives and their families. He listened until they were done, briefly answering some few questions they had, but for the most part held respectful silence. Finally, as they too fell silent, one mother who had been certain before the meeting that she would not forgive him, said, "T h a p e l o, doesn't your name mean prayer?" She then proceeded to speak as a teacher and elder to him, and along with the other mothers, embraced and granted him forgiveness.

Photo: Astrid Berg, www.astridberg.com

Reclaiming the Life Force of Accountability

This story of the mothers of the Guguletu Seven and Mbelo is presented as an illustration of a process of addressing betrayal and harm caused with courage and honesty; the mothers provide a sobering, yet hope-filled model for the possibilities.[2] Yet, the feeling of despair that may be evoked by approaching the topic of harm caused makes sense, for there are few good models of attending to and remediating harm. When reconciliation is not engaged, it frequently is the case that a particular incident or accumulation of incidents of harm spells the death of a relationship. The mothers of the Guguletu Seven and this man who was involved in killing their sons found their way to reconciliation. By facing the challenges inherent in exploring the harm they experienced, they were able to connect and repair their relationships. This work of connecting, reconnecting, and deepening relationship could be described as the work of *accountability*.

While the story of Mbelo is set in the dramatic and compelling context of the South African history of apartheid, the need for accountability is as commonplace as the disagreements, conflicts, and tensions that punctuate every sort of human relationship. When those in relationship do not engage accountability, whether it be due to lack of willingness or absence of capacity to do so, conflicts and tensions may dominate, destroy, or impede the relationship. Yet, accountability as a practice is a difficult task to engage. Even the word accountability triggers complex reactions.

Just as harm caused runs throughout the history of humanity, so do efforts, genuine and failed, for accountability. Wars and death sentences have been waged in the name of righting wrongs done. Punishments, large and small, have been intended to teach lessons and build character. Yet such moves toward accountability are not accountability at all. False efforts to do so range from punitive and scapegoating to permissive and codependent. Whether personal or social in nature, effective models of accountability that provide images of repair and reconnection and deepening relationship are hard to come by.

There is another thread which runs through history, bringing awareness that accountability must be relational. It is reflected in tracing the derivation of

Accountability could be defined as the ability to respond to relationships and obligations when mistakes and failures cause harm.

the word accountability to its roots. From the Latin, it is a compound of words meaning "acquiring the ability to reckon or think together with force"[3]

(*Oxford English Dictionary*). From this perspective, accountability could be defined as the ability to respond to relationships and obligations when mistakes and failures cause harm. Parallel to the vengeful and punitive actions within cultures have also been practices geared toward recognition and repair of harm to relationships among and between individuals and group, humans and others, divine and mortal.

Cultural Models of Accountability Practices

The traditional approaches of indigenous peoples toward resolving conflict are often grounded in world views that value repairing relationships when conflict or disagreement occur. An example from West Africa is the ash circle of the Dagara people. Malidoma Somé (1998) teaches that the ash circle addresses conflict between individuals by bringing it to the larger group.[4] Those in conflict speak about what happened for them while leaders and other group members witness and offer guidance. If tension arises, leaders take it as an indication of need for ritual to heal past wounds.

According to Michael Cousins (2004), the Great Law of Peace that emerged out of the Haudenosaunee (or Iroquois) worldview put in check warring and feuding that was harming the people. Through the Great Law it came to be that a process of reparation was the most common means of resolving misconduct and conflict. The one who had caused harm and members of their clan would meet with the victim and that person's clan. All would participate in discussion to determine some reparation. After there was reparation, the offender was forever forgiven and the offense forgotten.

A traditional practice of the Navajo Nation, which is commonly referred to as *peacemaking*, roughly translates from the Navajo to "talking together to re-form relationships with each other and the universe," according to James Zion (Mirsky, 2004). A person recognized in the community for their wisdom presides over the peacemaking circle (Zion, 1998, p. 64). Zion (undated) observed that while there is respect for those who embody wisdom, authority, and leadership, and they play an integral role in the process, hierarchy and rules in the peacemaking process do not supersede the organic process which allows conflict and disruption of ties to be resolved through the idea of relationships and all that is brought to those ties. According to Tony Mandamin (2003), the process opens with a prayer. The participants include the offender and family, as well as the victim, family, friends, and community members who are involved or affected. Each person speaks without interruption about what happened, "how they were affected," as Mandamin says (2003, p. 3), and what should be done. In this process called *talking it out*, there is space and encouragement for the affective experience of harm caused and harm received because it helps bring the perspective of the larger reality. Then the peacemaker teaches. Drawing upon traditional Navajo wisdom teachings for parallels and lessons, the peacemaker contextualizes the current difficulties. After these steps, says Mandamin, the people come to consensus for a practical remedy.

In New Zealand, Murray Levine (2000) notes that a model informed by Maori values has been institutionalized by the government. This model, called *family group conferencing*, supports communities towards reconciliation as an alternative to punishment for offenders in youth and family court.[5] For the Maori, consensus is a vital principle and the plan must be acceptable to all, including the victim and the offender. The model is built upon an assumption of a network of close interdependent relationships that make up family and community. When that network of relations is weak, then the family group conferencing function is weakened.

This creative approach to justice arose out of an international phenomenon known as *Restorative Justice*. The movement emerged out of a tug-of-war during the mid-twentieth century between those who sought retribution against offenders and those, influenced by the welfare movement, who sought

rehabilitation for them.[6] The birth of the modern practice occurred in 1974 when two probations officers, Mark Yantzi and Dave Worth, initiated the first victim-offender reconciliation program as they accompanied two offenders to the homes of their victims in Ontario, Canada. As the movement has evolved and theory developed across lines of race and class, resources have included not only indigenous practices and values, but also thinking from many disciplines and professions. The critique that Restorative Justice theorists make of the predominant form of justice, which they call *retributive justice*, provides

Parallel to the vengeful and punitive actions within cultures, there have also been practices geared toward recognition and repair of harm to relationships.

insight into consideration of the practice of accountability. According to Howard Zehr, retributive justice is an "adversarial, authoritarian, technical, [and] impersonal process" in which "only legal variables [are] relevant" (1997, p. 70). It focuses on blame and guilt in order to determine the punishment that will cause adequate suffering to counterbalance suffering of the person or persons harmed by the crime. Zehr says that, in contrast, Restorative Justice is a "participatory [process of] maximizing information, dialogue, and mutual agreement" based on an assumption that the "overall context (is) relevant" and focusing on "making things right by identifying needs and obligations" and promoting "healing and problem-solving" (p. 70).

Restorative Justice was, in fact, a significant factor in the context for the unfolding of the process between Mbelo and the mothers of the Guguletu Seven. Despite controversy and criticism surrounding it, the South Africa Truth and Reconciliation Commission was an application of Restorative Justice which is the most effective and successful

model to date of accountability regarding mass atrocity committed within a country.

Repentance and Accountability

Additional rich sources for models of relational accountability are religious traditions. One example from the Catholic religion is the practice that is commonly known as *confession* and which more formally is the sacrament of the *Rite of Reconciliation*. The act of confessing one's sins to the priest is meant to symbolize reconnection with God as well as community.

Drawing upon Jewish religious teaching, Estelle Frankel's discussion of the Jewish practice of *teshuvah* is relevant to the work of accountability. Frankel (2003, p. 129-130) notes that the Hebrew word teshuvah is translated as *repentance* but the root of this word is *shav*, which means to return. She draws attention to the understanding from Jewish mystics that *teshuvah* is the innate longing for wholeness that permeates human existence.

Drawing on the teachings of the Jewish philosopher Maimonides, Frankel describes the classical application of *teshuvah*. The first step involves recognition that one has done wrong or that one's life is "out of alignment with their deepest values and truths" (p. 143). This is no simple matter because of the defense mechanisms that we all develop to protect ourselves but which also "protect us from painful truths about ourselves" (p. 143). Thus the work of recognition or acknowledgment to self of how we have gone wrong involves work with resistance. This work will allow movement through defensiveness and relaxation of defense mechanisms so that there is more personal insight and objectivity. The next step of *teshuvah* is to decide to change which, if potently engaged, involves articulation or confession of the painful truths about the self. Vital to this confession is some expression of regret or remorse for what one has done or caused. Such confession of remorse energizes change so that there is no repetition of wrongdoing.

The next step of *teshuvah* involves "the resolution to change our behavior in the future" (p. 147). Frankel notes that this resolution is shown to be complete when one enters a similar circumstance and does not re-enact the previous wrongdoing or mistake. Finally, when harm has been caused to another or others, *teshuvah* is not complete until there has been a making of amends to them (p. 148).

Paralleling these steps for repentance, Aftab Omer has described four steps in the practice of accountability which are: (1) to acknowledge harm that was caused, (2) to provide apology, (3) to provide reparation, and (4) to make a commitment to remember and prevent harm in the future (2002, lecture notes).[7] Omer has noted that the first step of this practice is by far the most difficult to accomplish and requires an internal process that could be best described by the religious concept of repentance. Considering the concept of repentance draws attention to the fact that effectively meeting the need for accountability is likely to be a painful and challenging matter which may seem difficult to impossible to accomplish. The process seems rife with pitfalls and obstacles. Yet, the degree to which one is able to engage this first step of the process determines how effectively one is able to fulfill the subsequent steps of the process. For without effective acknowledgement of the harm caused, apology is empty, reparation is inadequate, and a commitment to remembering and prevention is off-course from the start.

Barriers to Engaging Accountability: States of Victimization

Based upon my research (Coelho, 2005), a significant bottleneck to the first step of acknowledging harm caused, and therefore to the very process of accountability, lies in the experience

of the one who has caused harm being caught or overidentified with experiences of victimization. This victim-identification prevents a person from being able to authentically be affected by what they have done or to feel empathy for those they have harmed. Taking in the fresh experience of having caused harm is blocked by the reactivation of prior experiences of having been harmed and of trauma. In this way, one avoids and

Drawing: Mariana Castro de Ali

defends against the discomfort of feeling guilt and shame for causing harm, as well as the necessities for responding to the obligations created by that harm.

Identification with victimization has many faces and stances. Differentiating and naming victimized stances can illuminate this first most difficult step in the accountability process. These experiences of victim-identification could be differentiated as falling into two broad categories, unaware and self-rationalizing states of victimization. Unaware states of victimization are the result of previous personal experiences of traumatization and harm that have not been adequately attended or remedied. Unaware states of victimization may then interfere with genuine acknowl-

edgement of harm by keeping one from awareness or consciousness of feelings of shame and guilt as well as awareness that some harm has been inflicted. Unaware states may be further subdivided into dissociation, avoidance, or habituation. Through dissociation, a person is unable to track the experience of having caused harm because parts of the self are blocked or encapsulated. This fairly common experience of dissociation is similar to that of daydreaming that leads to a missed turn or bus stop. From this state, a person might say, "What? Did something happen? Oh, someone got hurt?"

An avoidant state involves an initial awareness, followed by a turn of attention away from the matter. From the state of avoidance, one might say, "I just think good thoughts and then it everything is fine. Nothing bad happened." Habituation supports unawareness by maintaining a partial or skewed awareness that dismisses the harm based upon its common occurrence. In this way, habituation allows one to avoid the impact of actually being affected by the harm. In this state, a person might say, "Everybody does this so it's not a problem."

Self-rationalizing states of victimization rely upon defensive reactions to the harm caused. From these states there is a feeling of being victimized by the other or the environment. One such state is described by Rollo May's (1972) concept *pseudoinnocence*, which involves a state of contrived innocence and retreat from actual power. From this perspective, the role that one played in enacting harm may be minimized due to the reactivation of past traumatic experiences, resulting in a sense of powerlessness and weakness. So, one might say, "I am just one person. I can't change a whole system."

Another self-rationalizing state of victimization could be described as narcissistic entitlement. One enacting this state tends to feel entitled or right in their actions, even if those actions caused harm. The other's humanity, along with their experience of suffering, do not have the same value or worthiness as that of the harm doer. This state is common in young children for whom it is developmentally appropriate that they experience themselves as the center of the universe. A person in such a state might proclaim, "What I want is the only thing that matters. If somebody else suffers, oh well."

Another variation of self-rationalizing states of victimization is paternalism. From this position, one justifies harm caused to others under the guise of knowing what is best for the other. A paternalistic justification of harm caused may use collective or normative standards to measure the other, so that the ways in which the other falls outside of the norms become the reason for the harm incurred. From this position, one might say, "It was for your own good. Maybe this will help you learn something about the way that you should behave."

Yet another self-rationalizing form of victimization could be characterized by the dynamic of displacement. In this way, one who caused harm puts the blame or responsibility for harm upon some other person or circumstance. The harm doer then distances from responsibility by claiming some extenuating circumstance, making some excuse for why they should not be held responsible or blaming someone else, perhaps even the one that was harmed. One in this state might say, "It is not my fault. Just listen to my reasons why. There was all this other stuff going on," or "If they had not hurt me then I wouldn't have hurt them."

Finally, another self-rationalizing state of victimization can be characterized by retaliation. From this perspective, the harm doer contends that the other deserved the harm that they experienced. In this state, a person enacts overt rage and hatred and demonstrates

intention regarding the harm that was caused. They might say, "I'm glad I did it, and I'd do it again because this is what they did to me."

Another significant barrier to acknowledgement of harm that one has caused is harsh process of internal self-directed criticism, hatred, retribution, and recrimination, which Omer (2000, lecture notes) describes as *gatekeeping*, those "individual and collective dynamics that resist and restrict experience." This harsh internal environment does not allow one to be affected by another. Instead, the person who caused harm may be caught in narcissistic suffering that does not allow an empathic experience of the other. Even though a person may recognize that they caused harm, their focus is so overwhelmingly focused upon their own suffering that they are unable to hold meaningful and empathic awareness of the other's suffering.

When any of these varied states of victimization interfere with awareness of harm caused or justify the harm done, then one is not able to be affected by one's own actions or the experience of those harmed. However, in order for a person to genuinely acknowledge harm caused, they must be affected by the experience of the one harmed.

The Promise of Transformation

It is likely that these various states of victimization, as well as the intense experience of self-hatred and self-recrimination, may be activated in the process of turning toward accountability. However, this activation of victimized states could actually be welcomed as an invitation for self-growth or deepening maturity. To engage the practice of accountability is an initiatory process. Another way of saying this is that working accountability is a transformative practice and a means of

participating in transformative learning. Such learning allows one to encounter and explore those aspects of the self that have not yet attained developmental levels of maturity. In other words, practicing accountability allows the possibility for working the learning edges pertaining to the development of the self through transformative learning.

For one who has caused harm, the possibilities for transformative learning are related to what Omer (2002, lecture notes) calls *imaginal structures* which he defines as "assemblies of sensory, affective, and cognitive aspects of experience constellated into images; they both mediate and constitute experience." Imaginal structures are the lenses, with personal, cultural, and archetypal facets, through which all experience is perceived even as they also shape and form experience. The states of victim-identification described above are manifested through imaginal structures that result in rigid and narrow patterns of response. Exploration of these imaginal structures can lead to deeper awareness of subjective aspects of the self that need attention and care; engaging these subjectivities with awareness can in turn bring about a lessening of the victim identification and deeper maturity and abilities for taking responsibility for one's actions.

In order for this healing process to take place it is necessary that the harm doer be sourced in what Omer (2000 lecture notes) has described as passionate objectivity. Such empathic understanding holds the complexities of individual and collective realities with wisdom and balance. Such a way of being with reality can be cultivated so that it becomes an internal resource. Most often, however, it is necessary to initially receive *passionate objectivity* from an external source. In the case of accountability process, this holding provides empathic support and objective awareness that includes an expectation that one will attend to the responsibilities and obligations resulting from harm caused. Passionate objectivity acts as

> # Unaware states of victimization are the result of previous personal experiences of traumatization and harm that have not been adequately attended or remedied.

a catalyst to help one work deeply and effectively with their own wounds related to past victimization as well as self-hatred and recrimination. This work then creates possibilities for stepping out of the over-identifications of with these positions. This deep process can lead to an inner groundedness, which carries profound attunement and connection with the wisdom of the universe and supports the creative engagement and participation in authentic practices of accountability.

Most significantly, as the harm doer emerges from states of victimization as well as self-hatred, that individual becomes able to be affected by the harm that they caused. Being affected then allows one to empathize and imagine into the experience of the other, as well as be open to their experience and willing to receive the expression of their suffering. This being affected and being willing to be further affected allows the harm doer to enter into a certain intimacy with the one harmed. Through befriending the one who was harmed, the harm doer becomes more informed and able to apologize and make reparation by having a deeper understanding of the dimensions of the harm. The harm doer is able to commit to prevention in the future as a result of exploring deeply within the self as well as with the other, so as to understand the blind spots and insensitivities that allowed oneself to cause harm. With this knowledge and understanding, it is possible to take measures to remediate these flaws.

Accountability Process for the One Harmed

Accountability is generally perceived as a process that the harm doer must engage. Those harmed, or those advocating on their behalf, usually passively expect the harm doer to fulfill accountability or they may take punitive or scapegoating actions toward the harm doer in the name of accountability. However, as inferred above, genuine and deep accountability requires the participation of those harmed as well as the harm doer. The definition of accountability provided above, the ability to respond to relationships and obligations when mistakes and failures cause harm, must be understood as not

only pertaining to the harm doer, but also to the one harmed. While it may be more readily obvious that the harm doer has responsibilities and obligations in relation to the harm that was caused, it is no less true that the person harmed also has responsibilities and obligations.

For those who have been or are being harmed, engaging a practice of accountability can also be a transformative learning process, an invitation for self-growth or deepening maturity that parallels that of the harm doer. In addition to the experience of being harmed creating an immediate experience of victimization, it also activates past experiences of victimization. The experience of past victimization is directly related to creating the phenomenon of victim identification. The added experience of current or recent harm provides the opportunity to explore the biographical origins of victim identification. Such exploration and reflection may bring awareness to imaginal structures that contribute to making one vulnerable to being harmed or that compromise one's abilities to create and maintain safety for one's self. There may also be imaginal structures that affect one's ability to minimize harm caused or to stop harm from continuing. In other words, engaging the practice of accountability allows one to cultivate personal power and autonomy and mitigate the experiences of victimization, past and present.

The four steps for the practice of accountability described by Omer are those to be taken by the party who caused harm. Since accountability is a relational and interactive process, there are corresponding steps in the practice of accountability that apply to the person who was harmed. The first step for the one harmed is to acknowledge what harm has been experienced and that it may even still be happening. While this seems straightforward, it is not. For paralleling the process of the harm doer,

over-identification with states of victimization can impede this practice of accountability. Even when harm is obvious and concrete, one may minimize the effects of harm. Since victimization can evoke shame for the person harmed, not acknowledging harm allows avoidance of that shame. Admitting to oneself that harm has been caused may also involve grappling with self-hatred or self-blame

Another significant barrier to acknowledgement of harm that one has caused is the harsh process of internal self-directed criticism, hatred, retribution, and recrimination.

for being victimized, for allowing it to happen, or for being taken advantage of or fooled. Such self-recrimination and gatekeeping can intensify the shame of having been victimized. Acknowledging to oneself that someone has caused harm may also involve emerging from some degree of denial that the harm doer would cause such suffering. There may be accompanying disillusionment and the need for a process of sorting through idealizations of the very person who has caused the harm. Depending upon the circumstances of the harm caused, such disillusionment may involve grappling with the human potential for evil. In the very worst of cases, acknowledging to oneself that harmed has been suffered at the hands of another may mean coming to the realization that one has been looking evil in the eye and failing to recognize it as such. Furthermore, when the process of accountability requires the complexity of effectively meeting and defeating significant evil, there is peril that if one is not able to make the acknowledgement of the harm of one's experience, then one may be co-opted and become an agent of that very evil.

The second step is for the one experiencing harm to take action to stop the harm from continuing. In addition to the obvious stopping harm directed at oneself, this action to stop harm is also protective of others. Through this action, the one harmed fulfills the responsibilities and obligations to those whom the harm doer may currently be causing similar harm as well as those potential others that may be harmed in the future. Some stumbling blocks for fulfilling this step may include learned helplessness, fear of further harm or retaliation, pseudoinnocence, codependence, and fear of losing control.

Learned helplessness results from ongoing victimization that creates a pervasive lack of ability to act on one's behalf or get the help that is needed in order to stop one's continued victimization and harm even when possibilities arise. In a state of pseudoinnocent victimization, one does not take powerful and assertive action on one's own behalf. Instead, one may feign purity or pull for protection or special consideration by exuding innocence or helplessness. One may defer to others as being more powerful and so more responsible than oneself. From a codependent state of victimization, one does not take action, thinking it might hurt or burden the harm doer. Another state involving the fear of losing control causes one to avoid confrontation because of the possibilities of the intense affective experiences that may erupt. There may also be fear of causing harm to the other. This step may also evoke intense internal gatekeeping. Self-hatred may paralyze the person who has been or is being harmed. The internal gatekeeping voices may ring out such condemnations as, "You deserve everything you get," or "You're nothing," or "Who are you to say any such thing to him? He's way more important than you."

The next step is to communicate to the one who caused harm that they have done so. This communication may likely involve an exploration of the victim-identification for both the one harmed and the harm-doer. This step may present great challenge for the one harmed, particularly if there are power imbalances between them and the harm doer. There may be fear that further harm may be perpetrated in the process of communication. Self-hatred for having allowed one's self to be mistreated may become amplified even at the consideration of facing the harm doer. There is also a danger that the one harmed may assume that the harm doer should know what happened. However, this is problematic since there were likely to be imaginal structures at play for the harm doer which distort or blind the harm doer from perceiving the depths and nuances of the harm that may have occurred.

The final step is that the one harmed must engage in a process of discerning the authenticity of apology and the effectiveness of reparation. This step

When all parties engage in a practice of accountability that is dialectical and inclusive of deep reflection, it is transformative individually and collectively.

requires passionate objectivity for both the self as well as the other, the harm doer, in order to avoid retaliatory and punitive expectations and requirements.

Accountability Within Community

One of the significant contributions of the Restorative Justice movement is that it stands as a reminder that community is a player or "stakeholder", in Howard Zehr's (1997) words, when harm is caused. While the personal and intimate aspects of this relationship are forgotten in the legal proceedings of the court, even within the current mainstream legal system there is some indication that harm reaches beyond the particular individuals involved, as crime is described as being committed against the State. In fact, community is a powerful player in many scenarios involving harm done. For harm caused to an individual or subgroup ripples into the community, so that it is most likely that the community also experiences harm. Furthermore, community may bear some responsibility for the harm that was caused in failing to provide adequate protection or in ignoring circumstances that led to the harm. From the orientation of accountability that builds intimacy and connectivity, the community is an active participant in the process of accountability, with responsibilities for action as well as needs for healing and deepening. These responsibilities and needs run parallel to the steps of accountability for both the harm doer and the one that was harmed that were mentioned above. Thus, a process that is held and worked deeply within community that is engaged and aware, will involve multi-directional implementation of both sets of the steps of accountability mentioned.

Accountability as a Practice of Intimacy

Relationships with other humans as well as with the self and with all of nature are the very substance of life. Without these relationships life lacks meaning and potential. Yet, relationships are fragile and easily damaged or lost. Accountability is a necessity if relationships are to continue to deepen and serve life. Barriers to accountability are created by joint biographies as well as historical and cultural contexts of all those involved and contribute to states of victimization for both those harmed as well as those causing harm. Thus, when all parties engage in a practice of accountability that is dialectical and inclusive of deep reflection, it is transformative individually and collectively. Individual maturity and wisdom deepen and collectives, be they dyads, families, groups, organizations, or even much larger groups, become more effectively functioning communities which reflect values of interdependence, collaboration, and caring mutuality.

Accountability requires that parties stay in contact at that very time when the inclination may be to retreat or sever connections. When connections are not completely broken, there may be areas of relationship that become off limits due to neglected accountability work. Yet life asserts itself through our longings and even our resentment.

and grudges. The ways that betrayal weighs on us is an invitation to engage in accountability with another in a dance that may start out with anger, fear, and shame. Yet, throughout, this is a dance of intimacy that with perseverance will result in deeper connection with the other as well as with the self. Just as certain seeds do not germinate except through exposure to intense fire, it is through just such work that certain potentials of the human soul may begin to unfold into being.

Notes

[1] The other officer who applied for amnesty was a white man who would not admit that the seven young men killed were anything but terrorists as proclaimed by the Apartheid government in 1986. He completed the lengthy TRC application for amnesty which required as much detail as could be recalled in recounting all of his acts of violence against others, and he participated in a hearing before the commission which was attended by the mothers of the Guguletu Seven.

[2] This remarkable story was an inspiration to me as I engaged the process of my doctoral project. (Portions of this article are drawn from that research.)

[3] This word comes from a compound of three others derived from Latin through French. In Latin, *ac* means "to accede or acquire." Ibility is from the Latin word, *ibilitat*, which means "ability." The Latinate word *count*, which is the root of the word "accountability", takes a more winding path on its way to the English language. Its root is from the Latin word, *computum*, which means "a reckoning." This Latin word is a derivative of another Latin word, *computare*, which as mentioned in the text, means "thinking together in a way that is intensely relational." *Computare* is itself a compound of *com* and *putare*. Com means "with, together, or in association with" and conveys intensive force. *Putare* means "to think together."

[4] According to Somé, those persons who are in conflict sit facing each other inside a circle that is delineated with ash. Starting with the offended party, they each speak their version of the story to a divine presence, describing what happened and how they felt. The leader and other witnesses may offer guidance as the stories are told. As need indicates, the group may then form separate circles around each person and provide appropriate recognition, mirroring, and encouragement to the persons in conflict which focuses on the value of each person to the collective and not about the particulars of the conflict. If there is tension between the persons, then there is ritual to heal any past woundings. Such ritual is determined by the village members and leader who carefully listened for clues about additional healing and cleansing rituals that may be needed in order to tend to past issues that are influencing the present. If tension persists, then it is determined that the persons involved are not doing their part to work things out and the elders then give feedback about that failure. (See pages 88-89 and 305-306.)

[5] Levine notes that the Maori hold that the primary responsibility for children reaches beyond biological parents to include extended family as well as the wider community of clan or tribe. The people included in a conference are the coordinator, the offender and family, as well as their attorney and a police representative, but also the victim, and their family and friends. During the process there is a time set aside for the offender and family (as the Maori broadly understand it) to meet privately to develop a plan for addressing the issues at hand. Others may be included only if invited by the family.

[6] This brief synopsis of the history of Restorative Justice is drawn from the following: John Braithwaite, *Restorative Justice and Responsive Regulation* (New York: Oxford University Press, 2002); Gordon Bazemore & Mara Schiff, "What and Why Now: Understanding Restorative Justice" in *Restorative Community Justice: Repairing Harm and Transforming Communities*, eds. Gordon Bazemore and Mara Schiff (Cincinnati, OH: Anderson Publishing Company, 2001) 21-26; Howard Zehr, "Restorative Justice: The Concept," Corrections Today, December 1997, 68-70.

[7] Aftab Omer was the advisor for my dissertation and a significant influence in my decision to explore the topic of psychological accountability. His theory, called Imaginal Transformation Praxis, formed the theoretical underpinnings of my work.

References

Bazemore, G. & Schiff, M, (Eds.). (2001). *Restorative Community Justice: Repairing Harm and Transforming Communities*. Cincinnati, OH: Anderson Publishing Company.

Braithwaite, J. (2002). *Restorative Justice and Responsive Regulation*. New York: Oxford University Press.

Coelho, A. (2005). *The erotics of accountability: Towards truth and intimacy in relationship* (Unpublished doctoral dissertation). Meridian University, formerly known as the Institute of Imaginal Studies, Petaluma, CA.

Cousins, M. (2004). Aboriginal justice: a Haudenosaunee approach. *Justice as Healing*, 9(1). www.usak.ca/nativelaw/ publications/ jah/JAH _Vol9_No1.pdf.

Frankel, E. (2003). *Sacred therapy: Jewish spiritual teachings on emotional healing and inner wholeness*. Boston: Shambhala Publications.

Levine, M. (2000) The family group conference in the New Zealand children, young persons, and their families act of 1989: review and evaluation. B*ehavioral Sciences and the Law, 18*, 517-521.

Mandamin, L. S. T. (2003) Peacemaking and the Tsuu T'ina court. *Justice as Healing 8*, (1).

May, R. (1972) *Power and innocence: a search for the sources of violence*. New York: W. W. Norton.

Mirsky, L. (2004) Restorative justice practices of Native American first nation and other indigenous people of north America: part one. *Restorative Practices E Forum*, 4. http://www. realjustice.org/library/natjust1.html

Oxford English Dictionary (2d ed.). s.v. "accountability." Oxford: Oxford University Press.

Reid, F. & Hoffman, D. (Directors) (1997). *Long night's journey into day: South Africa's search for truth and reconciliation* [videocassette]. Berkeley, CA: Iris Films.

Somé, M. (1998). *The healing wisdom of Africa: finding life purpose through nature, ritual, and community*. New York: Jeremy P. Tarcher/ Putnam.

Zehr, H. (1997, December). Restorative justice: the concept. *Corrections Today*, 68-70.

Zion, J. (1998). Dynamics of Navajo peacemaking. *Journal of Contemporary Criminal Justice, 14* (1).

Zion, J. (undated). Punishment versus healing: how does traditional Indian law work? Native Law Centre of Canada, www. usask.ca/nativelaw/ publications/jah/1997/ Punsihment_vs_Healing.pdf

Engaging Images of Evil: An Imaginal Approach to Historical Trauma

Lisa Herman

What happens when an historical event, i.e. an event that is not only personal but also shared by a community, recedes into the past? What happens when we who were not there are still influenced by its images? What happens when we continue to be traumatized by the images of that event (and other events)? Does it make a difference whether we are conscious of the effects and whether we are not? How do we become aware of the event's present effect on us? Known in the psy-

Lisa Herman, Ph.D., MFT, REAT is a Marriage and Family Therapist and Registered Expressive Arts Therapist practicing in Monterey, California. She received her Masters Degree in Educational Psychology from California State University, Hayward and her Ph.D. in Integral Studies from the California Institute of Integral Studies in San Francisco. Her dissertation topic was: Engaging the Images of Evil. She has taught at CIIS, the European Graduate School in Switzerland and ISIS (Institute for Interdisciplinary Studies)-Israel. She is now teaching at the Institute of Transpersonal Psychology in Palo Alto where she is Executive Core Faculty and Director, Creative Expression, as well as the Institute of Imaginal Studies, recently renamed Meridian University. Lisa lived in both Canada, where she was acting co-director, taught and still teaches for ISIS-Canada and Israel where she had a private practice. She has worked in community agencies for many years, including schools, hospitals, mental health facilities, women's organizations and prisons, and she has presented her research and practice internationally. She is an accomplished teacher, therapist, supervisor, trainer and author (novels, poetry and professional writing).

chological world as 'secondary trauma' this ongoing presence of particular historical events is my area of research, research that occurs in the imagination of a non-participant to that event. My particular concern is the effect of the images of evil events and their iconic manifestation: Auschwitz.

Imaginal psychology's focus is the soul and how we can allow ourselves to open to soul's experience. We know that the project for increasing our capacities to soul's experience precludes knowing what will come. This staying open to outcome means we must be ready for all possibilities. Joy and goodness are surely out there for us. Sorrow and evil are also. By opening to all experience in the imagination, we can then allow conscious shaping for what we bring to the world. We can increase joy by maintaining a sense of hope that we are evolving into more enlightened beings and that our planet will survive. We can concurrently recognize what we are capable of doing to destroy life and nur-

> ## Does art … have a special responsibility with respect to traumatic events that remain invested with value and emotion? (Capra, 1999)

ture our own abilities to recognize and challenge evil. The images of evil call for our engagement. I contend that if we do not become aware of the call and respond appropriately, they will evolve on their own and continue to find yet new perpetrators inspiring us to yet more horrible action.

How does a non-participant in an historical event engage with the disturbing images of evil inspired by that event? We engage by participating with the images in the liminal space between history and imagination – the place where the images live. (This is not archetypal space where images are accessed in a more rigid cultural context, but a transformative space where images co-create something new with human participation.) A traditional way to access the liminal is through the arts. Imaginal psychologist Aftab Ome postulates that it is wise to experience before explaining (2003, personal communication). I offer below my experience of artfully engaging Auschwitz images in liminal space and then wil offer a theoretical construct for containing the 'unimaginable' as some scholars now designate the Holocaust.

When is Auschwitz?

One cold week in November, I went on a meditation retreat to the international historical site of the concentration camp near Krakow, Poland, known as Auschwitz. The last day I wandered alone to the far reaches of the extermination camp. Down a tree-lined path I found the ruins of a crematorium that was not blown up like the others by the retreating Nazis, but rather by the inmates – the Sonderkommando. These were prisoners who had been chosen under threat of death to staff the apparatus for the gassing of the victims and disposal of their bodies. Women inmates had smuggled the Sonderkommando explosives to blow up the building. All these prisoners were later executed for their acts. This particular place of fallen bricks and ashes feels different to me than the others – as if I can experience the rebels' resistance in the rubble. I am less sad at this site. I feel pride and anger and gratitude to these people who resisted, as if this would have been my choice. I kneel and say "thank-you", thinking I wouldn't have had the courage to be one of them. I walk on. I walk on down the gravel road and encounter a display case under glass. Three photos show women's bodies being flung into a fire-pit. The sign says, "Here the Greek Jew Alex took photos of corpses burning." My son told me later he heard that women's body fat helped the fire burn hotter. I wonder, how did Alex get a camera? I've read somewhere the photos were smuggled to the outside. Alex is long dead in the camp and with no last name lives in these images. I remember my paternal grandmother's maiden name was 'Elias' which is a Greek Jewish name. Maybe we lost family in Auschwitz and maybe Alex was one of them. There are no records of my family from before the war. Her married name was changed at Ellis Island and I haven't been able to trace from before that. I arrive in my walk to the asshole of Auschwitz, the very back, and a vast open field with a few round buildings. The sign here says in Polish, Hebrew and English:

> The pools and round buildings in view are a group of a (sic) sewage plants built for the constantly rising number of prisoners brought to the camp reaching 90,000 (they were put to death after arrival – explanation mine) and for the *planned extension of Auschwitz*. (italics mine)

The planned extension of Auschwitz. What am I remembering in this moment as I type on my laptop? I remember how cold I was at the retreat and how much colder I felt when I read those words. How frightened. I am still cold and frightened now as I look at this photo and type these words. My body trembles and I'm clenching my teeth. My mouth is dry. I'm trembling at an idea… at an idea that was not realized by the Nazis… I'm sitting at home in California, looking at a photo of an empty field ready for an extension that did not get built but was planned, and I am sick, nauseous, not quite paralyzed looking at a photo of a sign.

I am not now trying to remember what did not happen to me and what did happen to those directly affected. I am trying to remember and feel how it is to be me now and to articulate the experience of how Auschwitz (and others' historical trauma) lives in/outside my body waiting for its extension to be built. I find that my imagination allows me to formulate my present-day embodied experience of Auschwitz. There seems to be no academic language for what I know and want to express. I research what has been done before me and discover artful modes to express my experience and I find myself positing an epistemology of historical trauma that will include me in it.

Artful Engagement

Looking for a way to stay present to evil, I engage the images of evil creatively to see what will happen. The liminal space between history and my imagination, like the actual death-camp, does not fit into a previously known structure. It invites an investigative spirit. When a disturbing image arrives and threatens my psychological structures then I must re-structure what I have known before and increase my capacity to contain the new knowledge. The arts allow one to do this. They give us entry into liminal space where we can encounter the images that pose a threat to our previous understandings and recognize our limitations. Artistic forms allow one to exit from liminal space and the encounter with evil and shape what is found there. We can co create with the images and re-enter everyday personal and cultural life where lived experience will help us and the images evolve into something we can contain and tolerate.

Historical traumatizing images are what are left to us by historical traumatizing events. Those of us affected by these images need a methodology for encountering them, whether we are therapists listening to clients' stories or passing a TV in a store window that shows an atrocity minutes after it occurred. Below an expressive arts therapist describes her experience of not being able to contain such an encounter:

Forever let this place be a cry of despair and a warning to humanity where the Nazis murdered about one and a half million men, women and children, mainly Jews from various countries of Europe.

Auschwitz – Birkenau 1940 – 1945

Plaque on memorial wall at Auschwitz II – Birkenau

Listening to the stories of the survivors from the death camps of Omarska and Manjaca in Bosnia, I heard of things I had never imagined before. My whole perception of the world changed. I felt in some ways dirty, my 'innocence' was gone; and now I was carrying the knowledge of evil. I have difficulty telling the stories of evil. My fear may be that I will contaminate my surroundings with evil.

All the pain and fear in me gets stimulated. A way of keeping control is to stiffen up and hold my breath. I can remember situations where I wanted to cry out: "I can't stand this anymore. I don't want to hear anymore." Being in pain, taking the impressions with no room to express the pain that is evoked in me, has also at times, lead me into exile from my own body (Mayer, 1998, p. 252).

This expressive arts therapist later found that she must tell her own story of meeting evil through its images and she must do so through the arts. She and her clients used body movement and drawing to contain what could not be imagined. The arts are a way to engage with images that disturb previous order. They offer opportunities to write/paint/dance/ make music/ dramatize our experience. We can express our despair and confusion and rage at our subject matter and at our own process and wonder if we are doing enough. We can explore our doubts. Are we making any difference? We can ask ourselves why we are doing what we are doing. We can feel inadequate to the task of engaging Auschwitz (and other evil events) and know we must continue. We can create work from experience and document the process. There is a need for new methodologies when engaging the Holocaust: for this "conjoining of the sacred, humanistic and technological" (Denzin & Lincoln, 1994, p. 583).

I experience the necessity to engage the images of Auschwitz and have developed a two-way process that works. The process for engagement with this evil event consists of two prongs: from the 'inside' towards 'out' and from the 'outside' towards 'in'. The first I call 'when Auschwitz comes to me' and the second is through deliberate practice to access its images.

Outside to In

The images of Auschwitz arrive and call to me and I feel a need to respond.

Photo: Lisa Herman

Sometimes I receive a photo from Auschwitz through reading the morning paper. Sometimes there is a review or an advertisement of another movie about the genocide of the Jews and sometimes it is an article about disappearing people in East Timor or Darfur. My clients and students bring me CD's to hear and books to read, as well as describing their own experience. Journeys to other countries present themselves for my investigation of acts of evil, and my family and friends say poignant remarks that lead me to an immediate liminal state of engagement.

I record these encounters in my journal as soon as I can after they occur and I paste the articles and movie advertisements and ticket receipts in a scrapbook. When I cannot record my experience in words, I draw with colored pencils. The

images arrive with varying degrees of frequency (more often when I am on the East Coast then the West); however, they are consistent in their demand for attention.

Inside to Out

I do not rely on only these synchronistic occurrences to engage my data, but also seek them out. I find access to the liminal and the images through consistent and planned artistic practice. Inviting Auschwitz, I look at photos and read poems and books and see movies and listen to songs and then sit in contemplative reflection until moved to respond. I also have objects that I have brought home from the rubble of Auschwitz and sometimes I touch them: a ceramic teapot cover a piece of a railroad tie, stones, a section of a circuit casing from the electrified fence some porcelain chips a splinter of wood. I open the bag where I keep these totems or read a poem and wait for a felt sense to take me. I try to observe my thoughts and physical senses as flow and when I feel a shift inside and outside of me – often it is a gush of current, a warm shiver of sorts, a different vibration in the density of space – then I draw or write in sentences or a poem or move without music or make sounds. I exit this liminal space and then reflect on the process and discover what I have learned from it.

Here is a poem I wrote:

Digging

Digging dead bodies
Who might prefer to be left

in buried pieces

I yearn to join them sometimes

I keep digging
picking
at old scabs til they bleed
red flames warming no one's heart

We are all decayed

stillborn to a time of no joy measured
on any known scale.

Why try? What for?

I keep digging deeper obeying unheard
                          orders
from beyond the grave
somewhere out of earshot where there are
still some small shivering strings of sound
where hands still write.
mind still questions.
Still digging
Digging digging out of the light

Wet muck closes inside of me
Filling my cavities   begging not to know
anymore

Digging digging out of control
I cannot stop digging
I will die digging.

I will live digging.

Auschwitz Now: The three iterations of an epistemology

Moving to reflecting on my own and others' research into non-participant experience through artistic engagement of the Holocaust (Herman, 2009), I designed a theory to consider how we respond to historical trauma. My intent is to lead the reader on a journey through the lens of the particular evil event, Auschwitz, and present a conceptual frame for how non-participants remember others' experience. This is an emergent systems perspective that shows how iterations of engagement with the images of the Holocaust reach greater degrees of complexity and inclusiveness of personal and cultural experience. As those of us who experience and engage the Holocaust move further from the event itself, our ways of engaging the images have evolved. Later iterations expand and include the previous ones. The latest iteration knows 'the planned extension of Auschwitz' is effectively happening now in our coexistence with it; however, not in the way the Nazis imagined – as a real possibility. We know we must co-create with the images in the present and work to keep the death camp in the realm of imagination. Where the next iteration of engaging Auschwitz will take us is not yet known. My research pays attention to the three iterations that have emerged thus far.

The Event

First, there is Auschwitz.

And there are those who were directly affected by it. This includes the deceased and living, survivors, perpetrators and bystanders who lived temporally and geographically through the events. They recorded their testimony in the moment through screams of pain and silence, rationalizations and explanations to each other, attempts at understanding and even forgiveness and often denial. They respond to their physical experience of Auschwitz.

Iteration 1

The first iteration of non-participants as inquirers includes those who witnessed the results of the Holocaust: liberators, front-line caregivers, journalists, diplomats etc. They passed on the story of what 'actually happened' filtered through their own present responses to the past. Survivors, perpetrators and bystanders can be included in this iteration as they reflect into what came before. These less-mediated presentations by eye-witnesses of the 'facts' are coming to an end as that generation dies out. Iteration 1 provides the experienced present together with the experienced past.

Iteration 2

Traditionally, the next and following generations of engagement with historical trauma consists of the children of actual participants, their grandchildren and great-grandchildren, etc. In Holocaust research the blood descendants of victims are known as 'memorial candles' and are considered to carry their own special burden of memory and experience. They and the next generations of perpetrators and bystanders encounter the images of the Holocaust through their personal childhood and family histories.

In my theory for engaging evil events, I advocate a category that goes beyond the exclusivity of blood to relate to traumatic history. My iterative approach includes those who are not necessarily blood related but who are psychologically attached by a felt sense to evil events. Those in these iterations are affected by images of evil and the images arrive to whoever is open to them.

Iteration 2 is an iteration of engagement that is more complex than Iteration 1. A member of Iteration 2 includes anyone who attempts to understand, identify or resonate with actual participants' experience. They bring an imaginative element to the engagement with the actual stories. For them, the information is accessed through images created by participants and the first iteration: photos, stories, music and other art forms. All engage the experience of others by trying to identify with them, i.e. feeling what Anne Frank felt or disavowing, i.e. "I would never have been

Photo: Lisa Herman

a collaborator" or embracing, "I might have enjoyed being in the SS". They attempt to imagine what it was like as if they were there, as if they were someone other than whom they are. Some act out their relationship to the images of evil and perpetrate and become victim to further evil.

Iteration 3

The emergent third iteration of recorders/rememberers of the Holocaust inquires how and why they and their predecessors are remembering and recording and what effect this has on them. They are interested in memory and understanding and if those concepts are appropriate. They engage through their own present experience in the world and their responses in it and do not aspire to be who they are not. They have moved more into artistic practices in their inquiries and away from linear language and the 'facts' as they explore.

In the following section I will present some of the three iterations' approaches to Auschwitz with the hope that evolution will carry us onward to more complex ways to engage evil events. Here is a sampler of the iterations

Iteration 1

"Every image of the past that is not recognized by the present as one of its own concerns, threatens to disappear irretrievably" says cultural critic, Walter Benjamin (1968, p. 253). I would add to Benjamin's statement that when an image is not recognized, it recedes into our unconscious and will be acted out without our knowing. Atrocity both past and present needs to be a present concern. Those in the first iteration believe they need to remember the Holocaust and it is their duty to inform us. They know which events come to public concern is influenced by the images that are presented to us. We are most engaged by those that '…creatively pop up in ways that challenge what we think we know about the past and how we think we know it (Zelizer, 1998, p. 2). The first iteration of direct witnesses can bring us the freshness of their personal experience. We listen to 'eye-witnesses'.

Those of the first iteration who conveyed images of what occurred in the concentration camps to the world were newspaper reporters. The prisoners felt sometimes silenced or were not able to speak about it to anyone who had not been 'there'. The journalists often had no words to describe what they were sensing. They could not understand it. Dealing with their own horror and at the same time trying to convey their messages, left the reporters moving "… rapidly back and forth between shock, disgust, and fear for their own health" (p. 71). Photography, which until this time had taken a back seat to written text journalism, now came into its own. Though also irrevocably changed by their experience, photojournalists, better than print journalists, could in visual images capture a less-mediated version of the events. The visual images became

Photo: Lisa Herman

universal symbols for the Holocaust and the atrocity entered our consciousness as truths of our capacities for horror. We were outraged and saddened and our ideas of human behavior were altered. We fell ill and had nightmares and other distressing symptoms. For a while, the events were consciously remembered.

Time passed and we moved away from those flashbulb photos. We began to forget the details that horrified the world. For most, this particular history lost its status as a present concern. We became concerned with universalizing the experience and rationalizing the reasons it occurred. We attempted to focus on a few good people and occasional hero and not the evil that lurked behind it all. We concentrated on what was happening now in our world and taking action where we could.

Iteration 2

When history becomes traumatic, those who stay connected to its devastating effects do not move on. For us, the events exist in tact in the present. They are a present concern. We do not ignore the presence of evil in our times. For us, Auschwitz is present today lurking in the shadows with evil's other manifestations. Like the iteration before, the members of the second iteration believe they provide some service to humanity by remembering.

For members of the second iteration, the engagement with historical trauma involves imagining what it was like to experience the actual events. When the Holocaust arose again to western consciousness during the 1970's, the second iteration engaging its images emerged as well. The televised Eichmann trial in Israel, the American television series on the Holocaust and its later broadcast in Germany as well as numerous other artistic renditions began to appear. Survivor testimony began to find an audience. Once again we were learning of the event through its images – this time with more artistic shaping. The second iteration began its inquiry into what would they have done under the circumstances.

This iteration attempts to imagine itself into the past. These inquirers question why actions were taken (or not) in that time then. Stories and poems are created on themes such as: Would I have resisted and why didn't they? Would I have joined the Nazi Party and wha reasons would I have had? How would I have survived a death camp? What was it like to die in one? How did it feel to discover one's own child while removing bodies from a gas chamber? What was it like joining a partisan group in a forest?

Books, films and plays are written by this iteration looking for reasons for what happened and for the choices made. What did it feel like? Songs are composed and sung and dances performed as if one was actually there. The morality of who did what to whom is explored, often separating 'bad' from 'good'. Iteration 2 creates artistic pieces and flocks to witness others' creations. And sometimes they forget to stay in the imaginal realm and, becoming literal, attack each other in the present. Iteration 2 believes remembering and honoring what happened is important to the world today.

Iteration 3

Iteration 3 grows less concerned with the experience of those who were directly impacted – the victims, perpetrators and bystanders – but rather more concerned with their own experience of the images of this evil event. They believe that the facts of who did what when and whys of history are important. Their concentration, however, is on how the information from the past affects their lives now. They focus on their own responses to the images of the events and look for the relevance to their own times. Scholars posit that direct participants, being traumatized, were absent to their own experience and can never really know it. The experience of the Holocaust is often described as inexplicable. The third iteration investigators work to stay present to their own experience – not to be traumatized - and are less prone to try to imagine the experience of others.

Holocaust scholar Berel Lang tells us "We do not live in a time 'after

Auschwitz.' We still live in the time 'of Auschwitz" (1999, p. 224). Third iteration believes in a non-linear approach to time for their work. Zelizer (1998, p. 175) calls this the 'third memory wave' where "Bearing witness... (takes) on a retrospective quality that (allows) publics to move back and forth in time, attending to both the atrocities and contemporary agendas: people remembering to remember". This is an essential step for the third iteration and perhaps for all attempting to find their in-the-moment personal experience of historical (and other) trauma.

Third iteration asks who are we in the moment of encounter with the images of evil in that liminal space, between history and imagination? How does the

Photo: Lisa Herman

encounter affect us and how will we express what has occurred? How will we help others to, as Rilke asks us, 'eat the questions raw'? Without our questions and inquiries, and then our expression and our shaping images of historically evil events for others to behold, the images of evil continue to fester and find unconscious avenues to poison us and be literally acted out.

Third iteration wants to know how do we remember and present an event at which we were not present, this being our "preeminent reality now, no less than the Holocaust was the victims'

preeminent reality then" (Young, 1999, p. 77). The third iteration believes they have consciously assimilated the historical cultural experience into personal experience and have learned a lesson or two. They are consciously not wishing to perpetrate and re-enact historical trauma but rather consciously wishing to creatively shape traumatic legacies into something new.

Members of the third iteration are personally, culturally and trans-personally and trans-culturally connected. They are not only Jews who have been affected by the images of the Holocaust. Many are inundated with images of the Jewish tragedy. They know the remembering of what we were not there for is a cross-cultural experience. Benn Michaels (1999), comparing present engagement with the Jewish Holocaust and Black American history, quotes Toni Morrison in her novel 'Beloved':

"A house can burn down," Sethe tells Denver, "but the place – the picture of it – stays, and not just in my rememory, but out there, in the world." Thus, people always run the risk of bumping into a 'rememory that belongs to somebody else,' and thus, especially Denver runs the risk of a return to slavery: "The picture is still there and what's more, if you go there – you who was never there – if you go there and stand in the place where it was, it will happen again; it will be there for you, waiting for you." Because Denver might bump into Sethe's rememory, Sethe's memory can become Denver's; because what once happened is still happening – because as Denver says, "nothing ever dies" – slavery needn't be part of your memory to be remembered by you (p. 185).

The images of evil events require the third iteration to 'play' with them. The meaning of play here is in the seriousness of spontaneous play where the work is not necessarily fun at all. Play points to the improvisational nature of liminal space between history and imagination where roles and expectations are bracketed and the openness to outcome is embraced. There are no proscribed rules of engagement in liminal space, other than that of understanding this is imagined territory and no permanent results will manifest within it. We are responsible to ourselves and to our community and the world for understanding the impermanence of this space/time. It is a time/space for exploration. We are accountable for shaping what will emerge out of it into consensual reality. Working with historical trauma we are asked not to mistake then for now and to stay fresh to what presents in the present, understanding that action should result from conscious human participation and not from literal enactment of the imagination.

Ernst van Alphen is an example of the third iteration engaging historical trauma. In his book Caught by History: Holocaust Effects in Contemporary Art, Literature and Theory (1997), he details his own story of growing up in a Dutch non-Jewish family where as an adolescent he refused to be impressed by the compulsory reading of Anne Frank's Diary of a Young Girl. It was invariably linked to the teaching of his moral obligations because of her and the preaching was a turnoff. Only later, living in a house he discovered was designed by a Jewish architect killed in Prague's concentration camp Thereisenstadt, did he become interested in the Holocaust and found entry, not through the facts of history and narratives of the participants, but through later images in art and literature that showed personal responses to the events. He then became consumed by what he labels 'the Holocaust effect' a phenomenon where non-participants have a direct experience of the 'Holocaust' in their imaginations. Van Alphen compares the Holocaust effect to trauma

literature on personal memories. In the literature, when trauma is remembered, it is not a memory of something. It is a felt sense [my words] of "...the abyss between the lived history and the frames that normally enable us to experience reality" (p. 59). It cannot be described precisely. And in the traumatic historical memory, says Alphen, We 'get' the Holocaust as it is in our own time and space of the now. Through art we "... get in touch with what cannot be understood (p. 176).

Third iteration members live with knowing the Holocaust is now and they must confront the unknown of the abyss. They are working to not be traumatized

Photo: Lisa Herman

and they continue to create.

Living with the Reality of Evil Now

It is difficult to live without the illusion of good always triumphing and the belief trauma is a thing we can overcome. But so we must if we are to truly remember and engage an evil event such as Auschwitz. We must not use Auschwitz as a comforting storyline of triumph over evil, thinking once the Nazis were defeated, light defeated dark and so we can always defeat the demons. Avoiding the horror of what was is a way of avoiding the horror of what is. We are often encouraged at official sites of remembrance of his-

torical trauma to feel we have escaped from and survived great evil perpetrated by the Other and to feel comfort and gratitude for the present. We are encouraged to find meaning and lessons in what we view and attempts are made to place information into frameworks we can understand. But we cannot allow complacency. In her book, Writing as Resistance: Four Women Confronting the Holocaust (1997), a third iteration writer Rachel Feldhay Brenner, reviews the work of direct participant writers of the third iteration: "Edith Stein (b. 1891) who was gassed in Auschwitz in 1942; Simone Weil (b. 1909), who starved herself to death in London in 1943; Anne Frank (b. 1929), who died of starvation and typhus in Bergen-Belsen in 1945; and Etty Hillesum (b. 1914) who died in Auschwitz in 1943" (p. 3). According to Brenner, these women used creative writing to:

preserve faith in the reality of a faithless world, to continue to love the world despite its lovelessness.. While, as Jews, they were condemned to isolation, suffering and death, they continued to see themselves as women with obligations towards the world... Their resistance leaves us with a complex legacy of searching for the meaning of life in a reality of senseless brutality, unimaginable hatred, and atrocious death (p. 10)

The third iteration believes we must engage with the disturbing images of Auschwitz in full knowledge of the worst we can do and not be hampered in our search. Our emotions need room to play – be they fear, anger or even excitement with our own carnal desires. We must not be forced to meaning and a comforting resolution, but stay with our experience as it changes and flows. Those who know a need to be in relationship with traumatic history that is not their own must investigate ways to enfold and integrate personal experience into past, present and future evil events. They must do this for themselves and they also believe for humanity: we must all learn to hold the sorrow. We engage in what Roger Simon (2000) calls 'this curious practice of Zakhor" (p. 19) feeling an *obligation to remember* [italics his] what we weren't there for and to express our 'memory' in order that our capacities for evil will be remembered by others. They want to teach ways that "simultaneously prevent forgetting *and* (italics his) making familiar" (ibid.). Artful engagement increases this capacity to "face (historical trauma) with our eyes both open and closed" (Liss, 2000, p. 125). We can distance and engage. We must not become comfortable with it. Our experience as it changes is honored as authentic and valid because it is our own.

The call of third iteration's membership requires entering a wounded space where we can respond to the images of evil. It is to enter with a sense of responsibility knowing we will return to our communities and, as after all rites of passage, bring our knowledge to further human creativity. We enter

> a new time, an interstitial time, neither mine nor yours; an extraordinary disjuncture of I and other, an experience of proximity that initiates an 'infinte distance without distance'... It is a moral time, a time of non-indifference of one person to another, of obligation and responsibility to and for the other (Cohen, 1994, p. 147).

We remember our obligation and responsibility when in process and when in return. We bring our entire selves to the work, neither disengaged nor disembodied. Through the creative process we engage with the images of evil and pursue knowledge through a co-creative encounter. By giving these images form to manifest through the arts, we help them find a place in our human-experienced reality. We provide them with an aesthetic presentational mode so they can be communicated artfully and it is our obligation to shape them responsibly.

> (Art is) thus a vital necessity. What Auschwitz has taught us, in fact, is that art is necessary for life. There must be poetry after Auschwitz, if we are to survive. And particularly the poetry which depicts mass destruction, which looks into the abyss and 'shows' it to us in all its horror.

If art was ever 'affirmative', it can no longer be so. The 'imagery of extinction' is necessary to enable us to go on living and make life possible for future generations (Levine, 1997, p. 119).

After Auschwitz and modern totalitarianism, the moderns' belief in the inevitable progress of manmade history was no longer tenable (Kearney, 1988, p. 186). Imagination provides a way to travel in non-linear time and allow historical trauma to manifest creatively

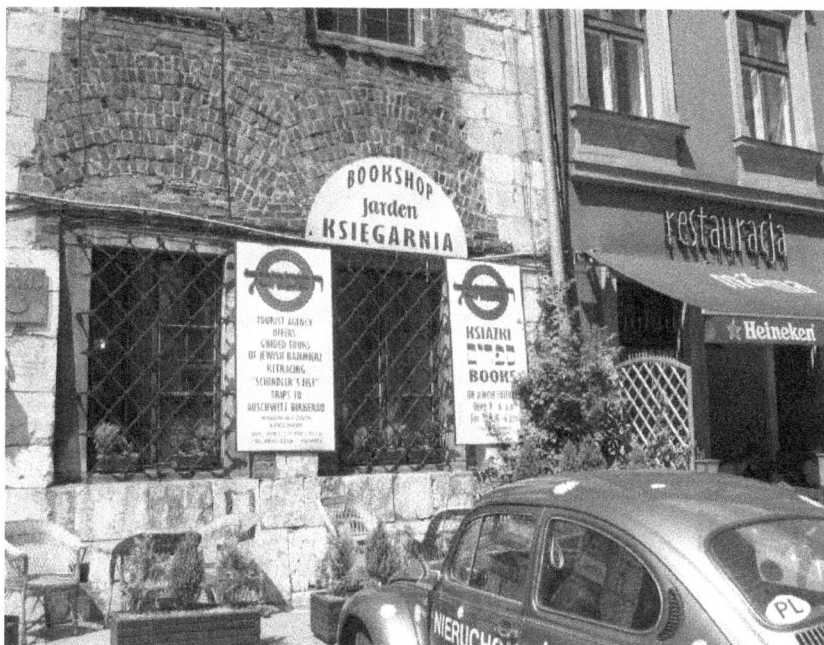

Photo: Lisa Herman

shaped in the present. We need to be able to hold more than one reality in this postmodern world: to live in the liminal as well as the tangible and to recognize the difference. We need new ways to engage with what was once 'unimaginable' and becomes imaginable. We need to engage in 'ethical imagination' to avoid totalitarianism. Fascism is a lack of imagination and "Ethics without poetics leads to the censuring of imagination: poetics without ethics leads to dangerous play" (Petraka, 1999, p. 236). For a sustainable future, we must have access to the imagination. If we are confronted there with the images of evil, we must work even harder to make poetry: to shape our experience for presentation both ethically and artfully. We must learn to live respectfully in those liminal gaps between the reality of evil

and its traumatizing historical events and creativity in the present.

References

Benjamin, W. (1968). *Illuminations: Essays and Reflections*. (H. B. Jovanovich, Inc. Trans.). New York: Schocken Books Inc.

Benn, Michaels, W. (1999). "You who never was there": Slavery and the new historicism – deconstruction and the Holocaust. In H. Flanzbaum (Ed.), The Americanization of the Holocaust. (pp. 181-197). Baltimore, MD: The Johns Hopkins University Press.

Brenner, R. F. (1997). Writing as Resistance: Four women confronting the Holocaust. University Park, PA: The Pennsylvania State University Press.

Capra, D. (1999). History and Memory After Auschwitz. Ithaca, NY: Cornell University Press.

Cohen, R. A. (1994). Elevations: The height of the good in Rosenzweig and Levinas. UK: Cambridge University Press.

Denzin, N. K. & Lincoln, Y. S. Eds. (1994). Handbook of Qualitative Research. Thousand Oaks, CA: Sage Publications, Inc.

Herman, L. (2009). Engaging the Disturbing Images of Evil. Saarbrucken, Germany: VDM Verlag.

Kearney, R. (1998). Poetics of imagination: Modern to post-modern. New York: Fordham University Press.

Lang, B. (1999). The future of the Holocaust: Between history and memory. Ithaca, NY: Cornell University Press.

Levine, S. K. (1997). Poiesis: The language of psychology and the speech of the soul. Toronto: Palmerston Press.

Liss, A. (2000). Artifactual testimonies and the strategies of Holocaust memory. In R. I. Simon, S. Rosenberg & C. Eppert (Eds.), Between hope and despair: Pedagogy and the remembrance of historical trauma. (pp. 117-

133). Lanham, MD: Rowman & Littlefield Publishers.

Mayer, M. A. (1999). In exile from the body: creating a 'playroom' in the 'waiting room.' In S. K. Levine & E. Levine (Eds.), Foundations of expressive arts therapy: the theoretical and clinical perspective. (pp. 241-255). London: Jessica Kingsley Publishers.

Petraka, V. M. (1999). Spectacular suffering: Theatre, fascism, and the Holocaust. Bloomington, IN: Indiana University Press.

Simon, R. I., S. Rosenberg & C. Eppert (2000). The paradoxical practice of zakhor: Memories of "what has never been my fault or deed." In R. I. Simon, S. Rosenberg & C. Eppert (Eds.), Between hope & despair: Pedagogy and the remembrance of historical trauma (pp. 9-25). Lanham, MD: Rowman & Littlefield Publishers Inc.

Van Alphen, e. (1997). Caught by history: Holocaust effects in contemporary art, literature and theory. Stanford, CA: Standford University Press.

Young, J. E. (1999). America's Holocaust: Memory and the political identity. In H. Flanzbaum (Ed.), The Americanization of the Holocaust. Baltimore, MD: The Johns Hopkins University Press.

Zelizer, B. (1998). Remembering to forget: Holocaust memory through the camera's eye. Chicago, Ill: The University of Chicago Press.

This article is based on research for my Ph.D. Dissertation: Engaging the Disturbing Images of Evil, California Institute of Integral Studies (2001).

Photo: Katrina Martin Davenport, www.octoberphotography.etsy.com

Of course there are times when I think deeply.
Lying awake at night,
In the center of the blackness which is night
Thinking of love and friendship;
Trying not to remember pain,
Trying simply to remember
And to understand;
Allowing all things to be as they are,
Untouched and yet embraced,
Intimate, yet forever beyond my possession;
Knowing the sorrow of time
And the passing away of cherished things.
Yes,
I attempt to remember as one who,
Gently lifting up old photographs
Of beloved friends
Maintains the bond.

      Michael Sheffield

Book Review

Bosnak. Robert. (2007). *Embodiment: Creative Imagination in Medicine, Art and Travel.*

London and New York, Routledge. ISBN: 978-0-415-4034-1

Astrid Berg

Years ago while writing my dissertation, it was the work of Robert Bosnak that most resonated with my experience of the ima- ginal—that is, that it is autonomous and has a mind of its own. I was pleased to be asked to review his book *Embodi- ment: Creative Imagination in Medi- cine, Art and Travel.* While not an easy read, Bosnak's weaving of theory, story and the actual practice of embodiment does stimulate. He integrates ideas from psychology, alchemy, shamanism, mys- ticism, physics and brain research as a means to theoretically explicate what he refers to as embodied imagination. Presented in a non-linear manner, the book may seem confusing for those not previously exposed to these ideas. How- ever, Bosnak adeptly integrates stories from his experiences using the embodi- ment technique to illustrate the method. Both in his writing and in the actual embodiment work, Bosnak holds true to a holistic way of being—that is, inte- grating various parts of the brain; mind,

Astrid Berg, PhD is faculty at the Professional School of Dreams and Embodied Imagination in the Netherlands www.dromenopleiding.nl and for- mer faculty at John F. Kennedy University and New College of California. After an extended traveling-pilgrimage-sabbatical, Astrid now lives both in the North Bay and the Netherlands and maintains a private practice in dream work and spiritual direction. www.astridberg.com

body and emotions; and indigenous and modern western consciousness.

Bosnak defines embodied images with the help of recent dream and sleep brain research. Solms and Hobson, while disagreeing on many issues, both come to the conclusion that emotion is a primary shaper of dream plots. In an article on neuropsychology of sleep, Hobson (1999) using brain imaging REM shows that the primary shaper of dream plots is dream emotion. In addi- tion, Solms (2000) found that the part of the brain that is activated during dream- ing is a region that spatially organizes information. In turn, Bosnak defines embodied images as "surrounding, imagined, quasi-physical environments and presences in and among which we find ourselves, presenting themselves as self-evidently real, accompanied by basic physiological processes" (p. 40).

Embodiment is a type of dream- work in which dream image affects are anchored in the body to be experienced simultaneously. Embodiment is not another method for interpreting dreams or other experiences of the imaginal. Instead, one works with the dreamer in a dual consciousness—the hypnogo- gic state (as when falling asleep) and the waking state. Furthermore, it's not only a dreamwork practice, but used with actors to embody their roles more deeply, individuals with PTSD and life-

threatening diseases in their healing processes, or as a method to incubate dreams.

The embodiment method can be used one-on-one or in a group. Since most of Bosnak's examples take place in a group, I will describe the method as such. Before the work begins, it is deter- mined which facilitator will take the leading role. As a means to become aware of one's body and emotional state before the dream is told, every- one scans their own moods and body states. The dreamer then narrates his or her dream in present tense twice for clarity. The embodiment facilitators ask context questions about how dream content relates to the dreamer's day-to- day living. Taking from the most sig- nificantly striking or apparently charged images, the lead facilitator will dis- cuss with other group members which scenes in the dream will be revisited and amplified. The number of these to be anchored in the body depends on length and detail of the dream, but the average is between five and seven. The process normally goes in the order it was told by the dreamer unless the dream has many challenging aspects. As a means to minimize fear in these dreams, work will begin with the most positive or safe dream image.

To begin, the dreamer is asked to enter a place in the dream environment. This process of re-experiencing the dream is slowed down to frame-by-frame. Coached by the facilitators, the dreamer enters a hypnogogic state in which the dreamer's awareness is brought to the details of the image environment, affective states and physical sensations. The dreamer is in dual consciousness—in waking consciousness narrating his specific image-feeling-sensations. After describing the bull in detail, the dreamer wants to become the bull. Instead the bull embodies her. Bosnak explains how he learned from Moreno that "characters inhabit bodies to the point of enactment . . . making it possible for the subtle body impulses of characters to fully self-manifest" (p.16-17). For Bosnak, the inhabitants of a dream are alien and have their own intelligence. Akin to indigenous people's and the European experience until the 13th century, Bosnak posits that we share the embodied condition with different physical and quasi-physical others. The bull is not a sub-personality of the dreamer. Taking from Corbin, the images are "forms of intelligence which present themselves as substantive bodies to the perceiving eye of the creative imagination" (p. 11), and not an irrational unconscious force to be colonized by the ego. Corbin defines two types of imagination—*imaginatio vera*, considered true imagination, and *phantasmagoria*, or confabulation. The former was a direct phenomenal experience as in embodied imagination, and the latter is "controlling, grasping attitude of habitual consciousness trying to figure things out to make them up" (p. 67). Using this method, one must differentiate which type of imagination the dreamer is experiencing while sharing, because confabulation takes the dreamer away from embodiment into cognitive thinking. This is an important distinction.

Also significant in this work is the simultaneous experience of embodied imaginations. Bosnak himself first experienced emotionally charged body-states concurrently when using the Alexander technique, which he's adapted for this work. The Alexander technique is a reeducation of the mind and body to change habitual movement patterns to those that improve ease and freedom and release unnecessary tension.

In the book, we visit a dream group in the Japanese Alps. A slight man, who recently graduated from college and feels insecure about his future, has a dream in which he is sitting with an older friend in a grey suit and a college mate in green around a table with a dish of fish. Across stands a 40-ish slender woman dressed in white. After following the method described above, the young man is guided to embody several affective states: the right leg with get up and go, the left knee of weakness, strength in the inner spine, sadness in the sternum, self-loathing in the hollow chest, hot anger between the shoulder blades, a sense of future in the tight fist and tears of catharsis in the eyes. The dream image-feeling-sensations are anchored in the body to be constellated altogether. This method detours from Jung's monotheistic compensatory nature of the unconscious towards Hillman's polytheism in which dream images are not constellated by a single center around the Self, but by many images.

Why experience so many states at once? Bosnak uses complexity theory to explain the process of anchoring dream images in the body. Ecosystems

Embodiment is a type of dream-work in which dream image affects are anchored in the body to be experienced simultaneously.

or her experience to the group while experiencing the dream environment. At a point when the dreamer is fully experiencing the affect, the dreamer is asked where it is felt in his body. After several moments of fully embodying the affective states and physical sensations anchored in the body, the dreamer is guided towards another dream image or experience. This process continues until the most significant dream images are anchored in the body. Adopting the words previously used to describe the image-sensation-affects felt in the body, the dreamer is guided through each anchor point. This is repeated two or more times as the dreamer is intended to feel all anchors at once. Bosnak concludes, "Experiencing an unbearable familiar state contextualized as one among a variety of related states releases the static energy, clogged in dissociated isolation, into a larger system as a quickening fresh circulation" (p. 134).

Bosnak opens the book with a description of a dream circle with members from different nationalities camping in an ancient cave with 13,000-year-old mammoth paintings. One of the participants dreams of a running bull. Bosnak finds that dreaming is an initiation process, in that dreams work on our consciousness whether or not we interpret them. Taking from Merleau-Ponty—that phenomena perceptible to the senses precede conceptualization and reveal a partial reality—Bosnak has the dreamer experience the dream anew to observe the phenomena that then reveal

The embodiment technique, supported by latest scientific research, is a means to reclaim body and its lost wisdom.

like the human body, have a tendency to self organize by keeping a balance between chaos and order. "When a system balanced between order and chaos has become too complex to remain in its current state, a *tipping point* occurs, at which instant, like an avalanche, a qualitatively different state merges from the prior overly complex network states" (p. 33). As with the young Japanese man, the holding of body-states simultaneously in awareness as his many stories converge in the body leads "to reorganization of conflicting elements into a more complex pattern creating more elastic medium" (p. 16). Whether or not this subtle body shift is felt during the moment, it will play out in day-to-day life. Two years later, the young man fills out his body and leads a satisfying professional career.

This method is also been used to lead individuals with PTSD to an artificial flashback (one in which he or she knows she is in a flashback) to find an image not part of the congealed pattern. This leads to a break up of the routine congealed in the flashback, which then releases static energy. The use of embodiment with individuals with life threatening diseases aids in understanding their experience from the perspective of the body and stimulate endogenous healing responses. Bosnak uses the embodiment method to help actors more deeply embody their characters.

In conclusion, Bosnak uses alchemy to illustrate how in the past imagination and truth were not mutually exclusive as they are today. He delineates the split between body and mind, led by Descartes, in which the mind became more certain than the body and brought forth in western consciousness a disembodied mind and an objective body. The embodiment technique, supported by latest scientific research, is a means to reclaim body and its lost wisdom.

References

Kaplan-Solms, K., & Solms, M. (2000). *Clinical Studies in Neuro-psychoanalysis*. London & New York: Karnac Books.

Hobson, J. A. (1999). The New neuropsychology of sleep: implications for psychoanalysis. *Neuro-psychoanalysis: An Interdisciplinary Journal for Psychoanalysis and the Neurosciences*, *1*(2): 159.

Photocollage: Astrid Berg, www.astridberg.com

The Mystery of Death: Noble and Knowable

Meredith Sabini

To call death a knowable mystery may seem like an oxymoron. Yet knowledge comes in many forms, not only the simple certainty of black or white, yes or no, but also in subtle and truly infinite shades of gray. Death conveys when it is in the wings via images, some subtle, some not. Over the years, I have witnessed death in most of its varieties: by accident, illness, suicide, old age, even murder. It's common to assume that ruptures to life and limb stemming from a tree falling, a house burning, or an auto accident could not be anticipated beforehand. Labeling such events "accidental" implies that they were random and perhaps without meaning.

In this essay, I will present eight cases—sudden and accidental deaths, a suicide, a murder, a near-death experience, and a natural death in old age—and discuss their accompanying reverberations. "Disturbances in the field" accompanied each of these events. These ripple effects manifested in dreams, synchronicities, waking visions, intuitive hunches, and power-

Meredith Sabini, M.A., Ph.D., is a licensed psychologist and founder-director of The Dream Institute of Northern California, in Berkeley. She practiced individual psychotherapy from 1977 to 1997 and now specializes in dream training for therapists and dream consultation for individuals and organizations.

ful emotions. The reverberations that came beforehand seemed to function as early warning signs that death was near. My thesis is that death is a field phenomenon registered in the imaginal realm whose shockwaves are perceptible far and wide, and that what we call an "accident" may be so only from the perspective of the visible, explicate world. Death seems like a boulder that falls into a lake, causing ripple effects both before and after the event.

I do not mean to imply that all sudden

> ## Death lets us know when it is in the wings in a multitude of ways, some subtle, some not.

or accidental deaths belong to a meaningful unified field, because accidents, in the truly random sense, do seem to occur. My hope is that the material presented here, gathered out of the painful soil of tragedy and loss, may provide a perspective on death that honors our fundamental human need to see meaning prevail over meaningless. Discovering these warning signs has left me more comfortable with death rather than

less, as if it were not necessarily the sudden and frightening intruder it is often characterized to be.

My first encounter with death's approach took place in my late twenties when my grandmother greeted me in tears one day, saying that Grandpa Joe probably wouldn't be with us much longer. She said he had been awakened that morning by a dream in which his mother was calling to him. I felt a chill and the hair on the back of my neck stand up as I heard this. How did my grandmother know what this dream heralded? Had she heard of similar dreams from other relatives? Was it part of her cultural tradition, learned from the priest to whom she told dreams weekly?

At that young age, I didn't yet appreciate how much we may know without being taught. Now more familiar with the vastness of our psychological heritage as a species which Jung called the collective unconscious and others call the imaginal realm, I can imagine that dreams such as my grandmother's are part of our ancestral experience. They are in our bones. Why would we not understand them? Human beings have been having dreams about life and death, telling them and hearing them, for thousands of generations throughout the history of our kin.

The next account is of a dream and an unusual event just prior to a plane crash in 1972 in which my mother and stepfather were killed, as was everyone on board. The event came under the jurisdiction of international law and was classified as accidental from medical, legal, and social standpoints. A formal, court-sanctioned investigation was undertaken to determine the cause of the crash. It soon was found: the pilot had had a slow heart attack and none of the crew noticed his error in activating the landing flaps during takeoff. Witnesses said the plane fell from the sky like a rock. These findings explained the proximate, physical cause of the accident.

I pursued another type of investigation into its meaning, and the search led to several specific prodromal or advance warning signs of death's presence. One was an unusual dream my mother had three times the week preceding her death. She told it to a close friend and, later, I found a written account among her papers:

A friend is hanging on a cliff over the ocean. I was too, but escaped. We are waiting for a rescue team. First the amateurs come—they laugh and don't believe me. I go on to ask the professionals. They are kind but too busy. No one will come. Three days, same dream, still waiting for rescue. I'll have to rescue her myself. I wake up at this point, agitated and afraid.

My mother's dream depicts her many attempts to obtain help in rescuing her creativity and full vitality, and how neither people at her church nor mental health professionals were able to get a lifeline to the part of her soul that was stranded. Many years later, while reading Jung's seminar on children's dreams, I came across a passage in which he comments that a dream where there is a seemingly insoluble situation with no way out does sometimes prefigure death, as it did here (Jung, 1938, p. 81).

The other disturbance in the field prior to the plane crash was an unusual emotional eruption in my youngest brother, who was eleven at the time.

The day our folks were to depart, he was overcome with fear and anxiety, even though he was accustomed to the regular business trips my stepfather made, traveling abroad perhaps once a month and often accompanied by my mother. As they were about to leave that fateful day, my brother, sobbing, begged them not to go. A reaction of such intensity had never before occurred. Beset with grief, he had to be restrained by the aunt who had come to stay with him while the folks were away. It was as if the veil had thinned and he perceived what was about to happen.

There was, of course, no conscious knowledge on anyone's part that a fatal accident was about to take place. And yet knowledge of an impending tragedy did seem to exist in the imaginal realm or implicate order, and manifested via her recurring dream and his intense fear. Though neither my mother nor brother could have explained these

Perceptions of non-ordinary reality are simply perceptions of the spirit world, and, as data, need to be subjected to conscious reflection and evaluation.

experiences, their perceptions were nevertheless accurately resonant with what was about to happen. Death was coming and the field around it was very active.

The next story concerns a colleague who suddenly collapsed of a heart attack and died. A psychiatrist in his late sixties, he was very active and involved in life. Just prior to his death, a younger colleague dreamed that she and he were talking, and then it became time for him to "go home." The next scene showed a huge redwood tree, felled (end of dream). Intuitively concerned that the dream might be foretelling his death, she shared it with him; she reported that a cold chill went through the room as she did so. After his death, others came forward with similar premonitions and dreams about him. He was a popular man with a large practice and many students and friends, so it is not surprising

that those in his kinship group would perceive the impending loss.

The evening before he died, he and his wife went to a Saturday-night film, as was their custom. On their way home, he commented on how pleased he was with life, in that everything seemed to be going well—his children and grandchildren were prospering, his practice was all he had hoped for, and he felt deeply content. Before retiring, he took out a volume of Emily Dickinson's poetry and read to his wife poem 1640, which Dickinson wrote near the end of her own life (in Johnson, 1986):

Take all away from me,
but leave me Ecstasy
And I am richer then
than all my Fellow Men—
Ill it becometh me to dwell so wealthily
When at my very Door
are those possessing more,
In abject poverty —

His train of thought during the evening took the classic path of a life review. The poem he chose to read suggests a willingness to surrender the wealth of the world for the riches of the spirit. He died the next day, which was Easter Sunday.

The death of Antonia Wolff, an associate of Jung's, also came suddenly and unexpectedly. Ms. Wolff's physician had noted that her heart and liver functions were probably impaired on account of her heavy cigarette smoking, but she was not symptomatically ill except for some arthritis prior to Friday, March 20, 1953, when she died suddenly in her sleep at the age of sixty-five. Two people who had previously been in analysis with her sensed the impending loss and made plans to meet with her. Jungian analyst Gerhard Adler arrived in Zürich on March 2; describing his hour on Friday, March 20, the last day of her life, Adler said:

It was one of those rare hours when everything seemed "in Tao." Toni was so near and warm and human…. We laughed a lot during this hour…. I went home full of the radiance of that hour and with a profound sense of peace. (Adler, 1978, p. 96).

Ms. Wolff offered Adler another appointment on Saturday, but, sensing that she needed the weekend, he declined, and scheduled one for Monday. On Saturday he learned she had died in her sleep. Adler's having postponed a trip to Israel with his family in order to spend these weeks in Zürich to see Ms. Wolff took on new meaning, and he later commented:

It seemed evident to me that all the hesitation about going to Israel was due to an unconscious knowledge and foreboding and that this had "forced" me to give up my journey to Israel. I knew then why I had had to go to Zürich. Of course, this may be an arbitrary interpretation of what happened, but can a feeling of inner evidence be so easily dismissed? (Adler, 1978, p. 97)

This describes well both the instinct to weave meaning into events surrounding a death and a natural doubt from the rationalistic aspect of the mind about this meaning. His experience of Tao during the session was perhaps a synchronous resonance between the completeness he felt within himself and that of someone on the cusp of death.

Irene Champernowne, who founded Withymead, an innovative residential treatment center near Exeter, also came to meet with Toni Wolff. She said, "I felt I must see her, with a great urgency. I could not wait." She got a flight to Zürich and met with Ms. Wolff on two consecutive days prior to her death. During their appointment on Friday, March 20, Mrs. Champernowne noticed that Ms. Wolff seemed ill; when trying to stand up, she had to steady herself on Mrs. Champernowne's arm. They both commented that their posture matched a scene in a notable dream Mrs. Champernowne had had two years earlier, which initiated a series of visionary paintings (Champernowne, 1980, p. 48). Jung used one of her images as a frontispiece for his book *Flying Saucers*, and quoted the dream it came from:

Two women were standing on the edge of the world, seeking. The older was taller but lame, the younger was shorter and had her arm under that of the taller as if supporting her. The older looked out with courage (I identified her in some way with Toni Wolff) and the younger stood beside her with strength, but feared to look.... I identified myself with the second figure. Above was the crescent moon and the morning star, to the right, the rising sun. An elliptical silvery object came flying (a flying saucer). It was peopled around its rim with figures which I think were men, cloaked figures, all silvery white. The two women were awed and trembled in that unearthly cosmic space (Jung, 1959, pp. 81-2).

I first learned of this story in a conversation with Dr. Joseph Henderson, who thought that Mrs. Champernowne's dream prefigured the departure of Ms. Wolff from the world, the UFO symbolizing death as an alien force coming to take someone away and Ms. Wolff's stance that of someone ready to depart.

Dr. Henderson had been seeing Toni for consultation during the summer of 1952, approximately nine months before her death, and he too had an experience that, in retrospect, seemed premonitory of her death. In the middle of a consultation hour, she interrupted their discussion and asked him to accompany her to the adjoining

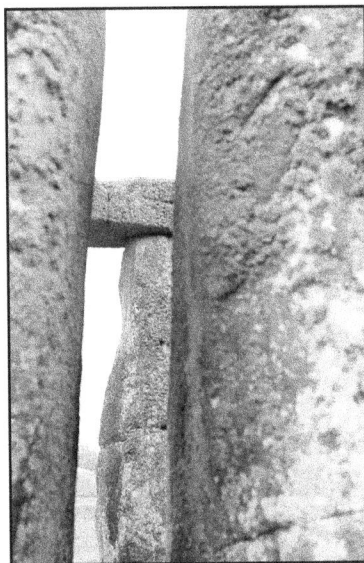
Photo: Astrid Berg, www.astridberg.com

room so she could show him pictures of her ancestors. He found this disruption highly unusual and out of keeping with her formal manner. Henderson came to believe she was acting on unconscious knowledge that she would soon join her ancestors. (Henderson, personal communication). Unusual as Ms. Wolff's action may have been from the standpoint of ordinary reality, it paralleled the sudden disruption of her life soon to take place.

Ample accounts of premonitory phenomena that demonstrate unconscious knowledge prior to death can be found in the Jungian and the parapsychological literature (see von Franz 1986; Jaffé 1963). Only a small percentage of the examples cited, however, pertain to sudden death, and the authors rarely explore the images and symbolic meaning of how death occurs. In the following experiences, the particular mode of death is prefigured by dreams, visions and symbolically meaningful events.

In the summer of 1997, Bay Area psychotherapist Zoe Newman experienced a near-fatal drowning; afterwards, she discovered that a previous drawing, a poem she'd written, and several dreams all depicted the precise scene. While swimming on the northern California shore on a clear day Ms. Newman went to explore a rock arch and was swept into a tunnel by a strong wave. When her companion found her at the mouth of the tunnel, she had no breath or pulse. Because of a riptide, it took twenty minutes to get Newman to shore and another twenty five minutes before a helicopter medic team was able to put her on life support. Her system had shut down and there was no heartbeat or brain activity. At the hospital, doctors offered little encouragement, saying it was probably "a done situation." Hypothermia apparently preserved her core, however, and Newman emerged from a coma a day later with out major complications. Two weeks prior to this near-fatal accident, she had had this dream:

A woman is in bed and my sister is monitoring her vital signs on a light board. Then I am the woman and I think about staying where I am for a day or two—I haven't made plane reservations yet, and I could go to see my father [who is dead].

In the next scene, I am in front of my parked car, walking up the ramp of an indoor garage. I am stuck, not knowing how to get further. A man behind me offers to help by doing the movement "pushing." I see a stairway and realize that is the way up. At that point, I see Al, who has followed me in. The other man disappears and I go out with Al.

The parallels between Newman's dream and her subsequent experience are remarkable. The themes are: being in a hospital, in a coma, with her vital signs being monitored. The indoor parking lot, Newman felt, "represented not only the interior transitional space of the coma but also the interior transitional space of both the physical tunnel I was washed into and the tunnel between life and death. I had been swallowed into its mouth and tossed back out" (Newman and Snyder, 1998). The dream mentions a possible visit to Newman's dead father, but "reservations" for this trip were not finalized.

Three days before this brush with death, Newman's friend Eric Snyder had a relevant dream: in it, a photograph of a group to which he and Zoe belonged was featured on the cover of *Time* magazine; the photographic image showed Zoe with her eyes shut as if sleeping. In the last scene, Eric goes to the funeral of a group member, and is shocked to see that in order not to waste the body, it had been processed into something like a can of kippered herring (end of dream). It had been, in fact, a question of "time" whether Zoe would open her eyes from the coma-sleep or if there would be a funeral for someone who had died somewhat in the manner of a fish.

Following her near-death experience, Newman remembered that a year earlier she had a dream about struggling with a death-figure under water:

A dark sky. I'm swimming in a pool and see a figure with scythe jump in and head toward me. I catch his arm and drag him underwater. Because I have been in the water longer, I have greater breathing capacity. I seem to last fine, while he becomes incoherent and docile, like a hypothermic person ready to fall asleep in the snow. I then surface with the scyther, to the disappointment of onlookers, all of whom would have been quite happy to let him drown.

Newman's drawing made at the time shows a female swimmer struggling with this figure in an embryonic embrace resembling a double helix. A struggle between life and death did take place, and she emerged holding the skein of a complex fabric that has revealed many strands of story.

The next account illustrates a similar pattern in which unusual experiences become meaningful only after the tragedy has occurred. Jungian analyst Geri Grubbs lost her son Mike in an accident that took place in 1984 when he had just turned sixteen (Grubbs, 1997). While trying to walk away from a fight among peers, he was hit on the back of the head and died instantly when his head hit the concrete. In the aftermath, many prior indications of his death—even its specific form—came to light. Mike's friends reported that for several months he'd been talking about dying soon, telling them that he had dreamed about his death and knew it would come in a fight. On the day of his funeral, his parents found in his desk drawer, along with other writings on death, a poem he had written that specifically referred to dying from a blow to the head in a fight.

Eighteen months earlier, Dr. Grubbs herself had a long dream about Mike dying: intruders break into the family home and hit the boy on the back of the head with a tennis racket, killing

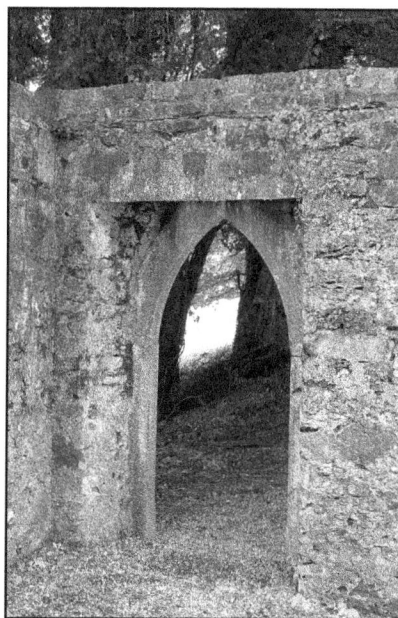

Photo: Astrid Berg

him. At the funeral, she asks if her son is really dead, did this have to happen, is it the end? "Yes," the answer came (end of dream). Grubbs first thought the dream was an image for her son's growing up, as if her little boy would be "dying." But she was haunted by an occasional, fleeting sense that his life would be a short one. When she once said to him that he had his whole life before him, they stared at each other wordlessly; she felt she was lying, but could find no reason why she would feel that way. Another time, she told her husband that Mike would not be with them much longer, and then wondered in agony why she would say such a thing. These poignant and moving recollections show how confused and disturbed the conscious mind becomes in the face of unconscious knowledge it has no way to understand. The adjective "prescient" can be applied only after the fact.

The final story I will present concerns a murder. The person who died was a fifty-three-year-old businessman who was vital, generous, and seemingly in the fullness of mid-life. I knew him through acquaintances, and we once attended the same conference. It was after this conference that he was found shot in his hotel room, having been robbed. His death came as a terrible shock to family and friends, and was called an untimely accident. It came to light that during a period of meditation on the last day of the conference, one woman saw an image of a skeleton directly in front of this man; she was shaken and unsure how to understand the vision or what it meant, and did not mention it.

In our culture, we do not have sanctioned modes of sharing such perceptions of non-ordinary reality. They tend to be consigned to the borderlands where they alternately may be degraded as wacky, flaky, or weird; or idealized as magical, mystical, or surreal. They are neither. They are simply perceptions of the imaginal realm or spirit world, and, as data, need to be subjected to conscious reflection and evaluation.

The image of the skeleton invites questions about the mysteries of destiny: Could this man's death have been averted? Was it, like Grubbs's son's death, "fated"? Would this man have been more circumspect after the conference if he had heard the vision? All we can say for sure is that an image of death was present in relation to him the day before he died, pointing either to an immediate event or a potentiality. Death did show its bold face; that much is knowable.

In his essay "On Synchronicity" and also in two published letters, Jung refers to "something like an 'absolute knowledge' which is not accessible to consciousness but probably is to the unconscious, though only under certain conditions" (Adler, 1975, p. 18). He specified that this is characteristic of synchronistic phenomena and is "not mediated by the sense organs" (p. 449). The examples I have cited allow us to modify this last statement: unconscious knowledge that comes via synchronistic phenomena may not be perceived by the sense organs in the way information is typically perceived from the environment, but may indeed register in affective and sensory modes.

These accounts offer only brief glimpses into the complexity of meanings that an encounter with death may hold. My intent is not to put unconscious knowledge in the service of predicting or avoiding tragedy. Though our human wish to avoid death is understandable, it is not necessarily possible. I think these stories show that out of the sequellae of tragedy, curious threads of synchronicities may emerge that can be rewoven afterward into a meaningful pattern, which may help those left behind. Puzzling and intriguing stories may come forward, as the ripple effects that may have originally registered only in peripheral vision can

Photo: Astrid Berg

shift into clearer focus after death has entered center stage.

This pattern pertaining to accidental deaths contrasts with my final story of a dying process that unfolded naturally. I was fortunate to have as a neighbor an elderly woman who shared with me her experience of approaching the end. At eighty-four, Peggy sensed that the dying process was beginning. She felt her body growing heavy, as if gravity

The urgent plea that someone not board a plane, the impulse to see someone right away, the shivers in listening to a portentous dream or poem—these are part of death's knowable mystery.

were pulling her back into the earth. She had classic dreams that she herself understood, such as a figure in black waiting at the end of a deserted shoreline. On hearing this, I reacted with the same instinctive shivers that I had

when my grandmother told me of Joe's dream. When Peggy told me a subsequent dream in which hands reached toward her, her own reaching out in return, I felt warmed, as if she were being welcomed and could herself welcome her fate. At this stage, she said she felt ready for the end, whenever it came.

This woman's personal maturity and lack of defensiveness enabled her to accept these early signals and bring her conscious stance into alignment with the dying process. She modified what she expected of herself, staying closer to home and resting more. She spent time sorting through the accumulation of papers and belongings in her attic and invited members of her extended family to visit so that she could talk with them about what they would like. By containing the transpersonal energy of the dying process, she was able to bring others into the process as she held its centerpoint. Her comfort radiated outward and helped others to be as comfortable as possible, given their impending loss. I am deeply grateful for having known this woman. Like my grandmother, Peggy modeled the natural ways we can perceive and accept the imaginal signals life gives off in its twilight phase.

I have no wish to critique the mode by which others die, yet I confess that how I die matters to me very much. I hope that I can prepare myself to meet death in as open a manner as my neighbor did. Death has provided many opportunities to practice by visiting me ahead of time. It first came on New Year's Day of my forty-fifth year, the classic marker of mid-life. Death arrived in the middle of the night. My bed shook as if there were an earthquake, and I bolted upright, cold with fear that the shrouded figure at the foot of the bed had come to claim me on the spot. I tried to bring it into focus, but the figure remained dim.

My visitor conveyed two specific images which I was instructed to contemplate during the second half of life. One was the surveyor's transit, known as a theodolite, a suitable pun on how God lights the way. The figure implied that the transit should be aimed at the end, for death was now the goal toward which I was to orient. The second image was a scale of justice with its two flat discs balanced on a center post. Death would rest a hand on one side of the scale and I was to measure all major undertakings by placing them on the other side. Only those with adequate substance would balance out the scale, showing that they had merit. I tried to convey the essence of this and two subsequent visitations in the poem quoted in the center of this page.

Though I was sorely shaken at the moment these mid-life visits occurred, I eventually realized that death was simply announcing its presence as a companion for the rest of my life journey. I came to feel that it would wait for me until the end. It gave me a way of making decisions during the second half, which I greatly appreciated. Considering how many of my own relatives had been claimed "early" by death—by age thirty, I had only one living elder—I had not generally been inclined to credit death with being considerate. But receiving this "advance notice" from a not-especially-grim reaper changed my attitude. It seemed quite considerate to visit me ahead of time. Perhaps if we develop the ability to observe and interpret the unusual phenomena in our peripheral vision, death's early warning signs, we will come to feel less taken by surprise.

The causes of death are often depicted in terms of the physiology of pneumonia, heart attacks, head injuries, and Sherwin Nuland's popular book, *How We Die*, provides interesting and detailed descriptions of these (Nuland, 1995). This medical perspective gives the proximate causation. In searching for insight into ultimate causes, we need a psycho-spiritual perspective. Jung noted that in the visible world, time and space function within specific given bounds, but parapsychological phenomena tend to relativize the categories of time and space. He concluded there is some probability that an archetypal situation will be accompanied by synchronistic phenomena, as in the case of death, in whose vicinity such phenomena are relatively frequent (Jung, 1958, par. 849). Death is an archetypal situation that, as we have seen, is accompanied by synchronistic phenomena in both the spiritual and the material realms.

Blackman's wonderful book *Grace-*

Emanations

Out of the frightening dream
Death stepped into my room
At night, at home, alone.
Death came to tell me it was there
And would stay with me until the end.

"Fix your gaze upon me
Weigh everything in my hands
For I am the koan of the second half."

Then death went on—one by one
It named all my friends
And made me watch them die
Ahead of time, so I would know
It would come for each of them
In their time, alone.

Past the circle I held myself within
Death moved once more, to all the rest
Down every street, it made me look
And those I never knew, I met
As I came upon death's social set.

Stunned by this final sweep, I collapsed
And fell into that place beneath the ground
Where Death's hand turns the world around.
(Sabini, 1993, p. 12)

ful Exits: How Great Beings Die, gives more than one hundred accounts of how Tibetan, Hindu, and Zen master teachers left this world. One can read about the last days of Buddha, Kabir, Gandhi, Rumi, Basho, Milarepa, Aurobindo, Ramakrishna, Chuang-Tze, Yogananda, and others. The common theme is that the teacher seems to know when the end will come, and meets it willingly. Here is an example: Kobo Daishi, founder of the Shington sect of Buddhism, predicted that he would die on the twenty-first day of the third month. As the time grew near, he reminded his disciples that he would not live much longer, saying he would soon "return to the mountain." One day, he refused food, sat in meditation, lay on his right side, and passed away. It was the twenty-first day of the third month of the year 835 (Blackman, 1997, p. 105).

The accounts of Eastern masters differ surprisingly little from those in *Apparitions and Precognitions*, which is based on Aneila Jaffé's 1954-55 survey done in Switzerland: A dying man tells his family that he "must leave tonight for a long journey," and dies at two o'clock in the morning; an elderly invalid says to his wife and relatives at midday that he would be going home by the night train at half-past twelve, and dies at that exact time (see Jaffé, 1963, Ch. 1). Though it is wonderful to read accounts of how spiritual teachers anticipated their deaths, I find it more reassuring to know that ordinary people like my grandmother and my neighbor can do it as well. This brings it within my reach.

When death comes naturally, its ripple effects tend to be mild. By contrast, with sudden deaths, the synchronous effects seem to enter the explicate world with considerable force. Von Franz gives an example of a sudden death and a dream of her own that illustrate this (von Franz, 1986). When she was about twenty-four, she lived in a rooming house where a sixteen-year-old girl also lived with her nurse. One night, von Franz dreamed that a terrible explosion occurred, and she and the nurse had to crouch behind a wall so as not to be hit by stones and lumps of earth flying about. Upon waking, von Franz learned that the young girl had committed suicide during the night. Commenting on the images of stone and earth in the dream, von Franz says that "in cases of suicide, the life energy is not used naturally [and] death is like a sudden explosion which dangerously disturbs the environment" (von Franz, 1986, p. 84). A similar release of life energy seems to take place with other forms of sudden death. By contrast, individuals who are able to prepare themselves for the great crossing seem thereby to contain the potent energy of this final transition.

culture's hubristic attitude toward death as an "enemy" to be warded off. We wage "war" against disease and condemn illness; we worship wellness and look down on those who seem weak. Who would consider calling death a "noble mystery"? I am not speaking, of course, of a romanticized notion of dying in a dramatic swoon or going out in the blazing glory of a sacrificial hero, but rather the nobleness death once had when it was honored in earlier times as a god—with temples, tales, and titles. I may have trembled down to my toenails on that New Year's Day when death

stories could be shared? Would this sharing help ease the guilt borne by those who had intuitive inklings or foreknowledge? Would a richer meaning accrue to all, by sharing and witnessing such stories? I believe there are ways that modern psychotherapy and ancient ceremonial forms could be creatively blended so that our experiences of the numinous could be contained and integrated.

As to the question of ultimate causation, the real cause of death, at least in the stories of accidental deaths recounted here, seems to be Death.

> # If we can tolerate the peculiar intuitions, the disturbing dreams, the spooky visions, or other unusual events that occur synchronously with a rapid departure, we may be able to gather together the broken strands and reweave them into a meaningful pattern.

Sudden deaths, with their dramatic imagery, invite us to wonder if the mode of dying can be imagined as an extension of a person's mode of living. We might explore the symbolism of a particular mode of dying as if it were a final dream. The Aboriginal Lardil of Australia, for instance, identify children by the place where their coming into being had been indicated by a sign or omen; likewise they identify the deceased according to the place where they departed (McKnight, 1995). We might refer to our elders as she-who-left-in-mid-air or he-who-went-on-Easter-Sunday, thus putting into images ways we can remember and refer to them.

When I mentioned to a friend that I was composing this essay on death as knowable mystery, she thought that I said "Death's *noble* mystery." I laughed, and said that her mis-hearing was wonderful, for it captured the exact meaning I was trying to convey. The word "noble" had not occurred to me, but it is a fine adjective. How in contrast to our

paid its first call, but since then I cherished that as one of the most profound experiences of my life.

Death conveys its mystery as a sudden intruder at night, a dark figure on a deserted beach, a skeleton appearing out of nowhere. These images may register in our peripheral vision, but we are unsure how to understand them. The urgent plea that someone not board a plane, the impulse to see someone right away, the shivers in listening to a portentous dream or poem—these are part of death's knowable mystery. We may gain comfort afterward when we can recognize them for what they are. If we can tolerate the peculiar intuitions, the disturbing dreams, the unsettling visions, we may be able to gather together the broken strands and reweave them into a meaningful pattern. Sudden deaths, more than natural demise, may initiate for the bereaved a process of reflection and contemplation on the mysteries of this great transit.

Might we help the bereaved by providing a *temenos* in which prodromal

References

Adler, G. (Ed.). (1975) *C. G. Jung Letters*, Vol. 2. Princeton, NJ: Princeton University Press.

Adler, G. (1978). Reflections on chance and fate. In G. Hill (Ed.), The Shaman From Elko (pp. 87-101). San Francisco: C. G. Jung Institute.

Blackman, S. (1997). *Graceful exits: How great beings die*. New York: Weatherhill.

Champernowne, I. (1980). *A memoir of Toni Wolff*. San Francisco: C. G. Jung Institute.

Grubbs, G. (1997). *By way of Gilgamesh: Transcendence and transformation in the dream series of bereaved mothers*. Unpublished diploma thesis, C. G. Jung Institute, Zürich, Switzerland.

Jaffé, A. (1963). *Apparitions and precognition*. New York: University Books.

Johnson, T. (1986). *The complete poems of Emily Dickinson*. Boston: Little Brown and Company.

Jung, C. G. (1938). *Unpublished seminar on children's dreams*. San Francisco Jung Institute Library. [An edited version has been published as Jung. G. G. (2008). Children's Dreams: Notes from the seminar given in 1936 - 1940. Ed. L. Jung & M. Meyer-Grass. Princeton, NJ: Princeton University Press.]

Jung, C. G. (1958). A psychological view of conscience. *Collected works*, Vol. 10. Princeton, NJ: Princeton University Press.

Jung, C. G. (1959). *Flying saucers: Modern myth of things seen in the skies*. New York: Harcourt Brace.

McKnight, D. (1995). *Lardil: Keepers of the Dreamtime*. San Francisco: Chronicle Books.

Newman, Z., & Snyder, E. (1998). Dream interweavings: Dance with the ocean. *DreamTime*, 15(3-4), pp. 24-27. Berkeley, CA: International Association for the Study of Dreams.

Nuland, S. (1995). *How we die: Reflections on life's final chapter*. New York: Vintage Press.

Sabini, M. (1993). Emanations. *Chrysalis: Journal of the Swedenborg Foundation*, 8(1). 12. Ephrata, PA: Science Press.

von Franz, M-L. (1986). *On dreams and death*. Boston: Shambhala.

A version of this article appeared in *Quadrant* vol. 30, Winter 2000 (published by the C. G. Jung Foundation of New York); it is reprinted here with permission.